Homeschooling for Unshakable Futures

Rise Above the Broken School System, Plan Curriculum for Multiple Grades, and Stay On Budget for a Peaceful Home and Confident, Future-Ready Learners

Jennifer H Johnson

Contents

introduction, to me

Have you ever faced something new and felt both totally ready and completely unsure at the same time? That was me the day I decided to homeschool.

If you're reading this, I'm guessing you might be in that same place. Maybe you've been thinking about homeschooling for years, months or just days. Maybe the decision came suddenly after seeing what school looked like during COVID or what's happening to the culture of our school. Whatever brought you here, I want to tell you right away... YOU ARE NOT ALONE. You have what it takes to do this. I PROMISE!

When the world shut down, I watched my children learn through screens and worksheets. I saw the strain in their teachers and the confusion in my kids' faces. That season made me realize I wanted more for them than grades or test scores. I wanted peace in our days, space for curiosity, and room for their hearts to grow. And protection from the rot I saw in our school's culture.

So, in 2021, I began homeschooling. Seven kids, five grades, one kitchen table and two make shift desks. It was loud, messy, and chaotic. But deep down, it felt right. Over time, the learning began to blend into our family life in a way that felt natural. It wasn't, and still isn't, perfect, but it's us now.

This book grew out of those first uncertain steps. It's for moms who want to give their children a better way to learn. It's for the ones who feel tired but still show up, who are willing to figure things out one day at a time.

Inside here you will find my heart, my mind and part of my soul. You'll find a mix of stories and practical ideas: how to start, what to gather, and ways to teach without losing your mind. We'll talk about curriculum choices, what to do when burnout hits, and how to keep joy at the center of your home. These are things that helped me survive and grow in this journey.

You'll also find honesty here. Some days, homeschooling means teaching algebra while the toddler paints her hair with yogurt. Other days, it's reading together in the backyard while dinner cooks. Every kind of day counts.

By the time you finish, my hope is that you'll see homeschooling differently. It's not about having perfect patience or perfect plans or being perfect yourself. It's about learning alongside your kids and finding beauty in the ordinary moments that make up your family life.

So take a breath, pour your coffee, and let's begin this adventure together. Your home is ready. Your children are ready. And even if you don't feel it yet, you are too.

Jennifer Johnson

Child of God, Wife, Mother, Homeschool Teacher, Strong Women

introduction to homeschooling

T hanks to what happened in 2020, homeschooling has moved from the margins to a normal option many families choose. The shift happened gradually as laws clarified parents' rights, communities formed support networks, and more families shared what worked at their kitchen tables.

Early on, most learning happened at home or in small local settings. As compulsory schooling expanded in the industrial era, home education faded from view. Late in the twentieth century, parents across different backgrounds began bringing learning back home for reasons that ranged from faith and safety to flexibility and academic fit. Court decisions and state policy updates created clearer paths for families. Over the last several years, especially after COVID, many parents tried homeschooling and discovered they wanted to keep going.

from normal to fringe to normal again

The first week we brought school home, I cleared a space at the kitchen table and set out sharpened pencils like little flags of hope. The baby was teething. Our high schooler had a history essay due. The fourth grader kept asking how rockets work. I remember thinking, *People have been teaching their kids at home for centuries. Surely I can learn how to do this.* That thought became a thread I pulled and pulled, and a much bigger story unraveled... one that started long before 2021.

For most of human history, children learned at home, on farms, in workshops, and around kitchen fires. They learned by copying letters on slate, measuring lumber with a parent, reading aloud from a family Bible, and keeping accounts for the store. Community schools existed in different forms, but the home was where skills, stories, and values took root. In the nineteenth and early twentieth centuries, as cities grew and factories set schedules by whistles and clocks, governments created compulsory schooling to bring order and consistency to education. Families welcomed the stability and access, and home education receded from public view.

It never disappeared. In the 1970s and 1980s, a quiet group of parents began asking for flexibility again. Some wanted faith to shape literature lists and science conversations. Others had children who learned best outside the pace of a large classroom. A few lived in rural areas where buses traveled long, cold miles each morning. These families wrote letters to school districts, met in living rooms, and traded photocopied lesson plans at potlucks. They did not see themselves as rebels. They saw themselves as parents.

Laws had to catch up. In state after state, families asked courts and legislatures to recognize home education as a legitimate path. In Texas, a case called *Leeper v. Arlington ISD* (1987) confirmed that a home school could be treated as a private school for legal purposes, which gave parents clarity they had lacked. Similar clarifications followed across the country. The exact requirements differed, notice forms, portfolio reviews, standardized tests, but one principle held: parents could be the primary directors of their children's education at home. It wasn't fast or easy. It was steady.

Culture changed alongside the laws. A mom I met in a co-op once told me her story from the early 1990s. She used to plan science labs at her dining room table and cover the beakers with a tablecloth before guests arrived. "I got tired of hiding what we were proud of," she said. Over time, hiding wasn't needed. The children of those early homeschoolers began showing up in visible places, spelling bees, robotics teams, college campuses, skilled trades, small businesses, apprenticeships. Admissions counselors grew familiar with transcripts built from portfolios, dual-enrollment classes, and community college credits. Home-educated teens brought work samples, reference letters from tutors or coaches, and a clear story of what they'd done with their time. The narrative shifted from suspicion to curiosity, and then to acceptance.

The internet opened the door wider. A family in a small town could join a Latin class on Tuesday afternoons, a coding club on Wednesday evenings, and a book discussion with students in three states on Fridays. Curriculum moved from catalogs to clickable samples. Parents compared notes in forums and group chats. Co-ops organized with shared calendars and divided teaching responsibilities: one parent ran chemistry labs, another handled composition, a third taught watercolor and perspective drawing. The tools multiplied, and with them, confidence.

Then came COVID. In a single spring, millions of families watched school happen from their living rooms. Teachers worked hard under impossible circumstances. Parents looked at their children's screens, the daily fatigue, and the noise of debates in the headlines, and asked new questions. Some families returned to campus as soon as they could. Others realized their children flourished at a different pace and kept going at home. In conversations with friends, I've heard reasons that span every imaginable line: faith and safety, yes, but also a child's anxiety easing without a crowded hallway; a daughter who found time for violin practice and advanced math; a son who finally loved books after switching to read-aloud mornings and audiobooks in the car.

I think about "Mrs. S," a composite of moms I've met. She had a seventh grader who devoured astronomy, a fourth grader who dreaded worksheets, and a toddler who refused shoes in winter. She was sure she'd fail at history, so she joined a co-op one morning a week and let another parent lead that subject. She kept math at home with a program that clicked for her kids. Science became a project shelf in the laundry room with labeled bins for circuits, seeds, and magnets. Was it polished? No. Was it a real education? Absolutely. Over two years, her seventh grader built a telescope with a 3D-printed mount, her fourth grader wrote the family's first "newspaper," and her toddler learned to match socks... a victory any parent will celebrate.

Homeschooling moved into the mainstream not through a single sweeping moment, but through thousands of small decisions like that: a mom choosing to read aloud at breakfast because mornings go better when hearts are full; a dad shifting his schedule to teach a weekly woodshop hour in the garage; grandparents who cover Tuesday afternoons so a teenager can take a community college class. It's a slow build, one routine at a time.

Today, when people ask what changed, I share three steady forces. First, **clarity**: families know the rules and can follow them. Second, **community**: co-ops, sports, church groups, clubs, and online classes give structure and social life. Third, **results**: children grow in responsibility, curiosity, and skill, and those outcomes are visible – to neighbors, to colleges, to future employers, and most importantly, to the families themselves.

I still set out sharpened pencils on Monday mornings. We still have days when the plan falls apart at 10:17 a.m. We also have days when the living room becomes a history museum, complete with hand-lettered labels, a playlist of era-appropriate music, and a very proud ten-year-old tour guide. That mix, the ordinary and the surprising, captures the real evolution of homeschooling. It began at home, left home for a time, and found its way back again, not as a retreat from the world but as a way to meet the world with rooted, steady hearts.

In the chapters ahead, we'll name the options available now, the legal steps that keep you on solid ground, and the practical rhythms that make this sustainable. For now, it helps to remember that you are joining a long line of parents who taught their children right where life happens – at the table, in the yard, on the way to the library – and discovered that learning fits there better than they ever expected.

definitions, types, and methods

The morning I officially filed our "intent to homeschool" form, I sat at my kitchen counter with my coffee growing cold. The baby was chewing on a pencil. My middle schooler was spinning in circles on the floor singing a song about fractions. I stared at that form and thought, *Okay, Jennifer, you're doing this. But what exactly are you doing?*

When I first heard the word *homeschooling*, it sounded simple, teach your kids at home. But I quickly learned it can look a hundred different ways. Some families have color-coded lesson plans and laminated charts; others read books on the couch and call the zoo a biology field trip. Both are right, because homeschooling isn't one system. It's a spectrum of approaches built around each family's values, schedule, and needs.

At its heart, homeschooling means parents take direct responsibility for their children's education. But beyond that, it's astonishingly flexible. According to the National Center for Education Statistics, more than 3.1 million students were homeschooled in the U.S. by 2023, and that number keeps rising. That's 3.1 million different versions of "school."

I remember asking another mom at church, "What curriculum do you use?" She smiled and said, "Whichever one fits this year." I didn't understand then how much wisdom was tucked in that answer.

Here are some of the forms homeschooling can take:

- **Traditional homeschoolers** follow structured curriculums, daily lessons, and grading systems similar to public schools. This works beautifully for families who like order and predictability.

- **Eclectic homeschoolers** (that's us) pull from multiple sources. We mix a math textbook with hands-on science kits, history documentaries, and writing projects based on whatever rabbit trail the kids are chasing that week.

- **Unschoolers** lean into curiosity. They trust that children are naturally driven to learn when given time and access to the world. Unschooling can mean baking to learn fractions, building birdhouses for geometry, or writing stories sparked by favorite movies.

- **Online or hybrid homeschoolers** use digital platforms for classes, anything from Spanish to chemistry labs, often supplemented by parent-led instruction.

- Then there are **philosophy-driven homeschoolers.** Montessori families fill their homes with hands-on materials, encouraging independence. Charlotte Mason homeschoolers read "living books" instead of textbooks, take nature walks, and talk about beauty as a part of learning. Classical homeschoolers focus on language, logic, and rhetoric the tools of deep thinking.

Most of us blend. For example, our home combines the organization of classical education with the gentleness of Charlotte Mason and the freedom of unschooling Fridays, when the kids choose what they want to explore. That mix keeps us balanced, structure for me, creativity for them.

Faith plays a central role for many families. In our house, we pray before lessons, and Bible study counts as literature and character training all in one. **I remind myself often that the goal isn't to re-create public school**; it's to create an education that fits our children – comfortable, growing with them, made with love.

I remind myself often that the goal isn't to re-create public school

If you're just beginning, remember: you don't have to pick the perfect method now. Try something, adjust as you go, and let God guide you. As Proverbs 16:9 reminds us, *"In their hearts humans plan their course, but the Lord establishes their steps."* You'll find your rhythm in time, and it will be exactly the right one for your family.

what you need to know, legally

The first time I tried to understand homeschooling laws, I opened a state website and felt like I was reading a foreign language. *Notification of intent, annual assessment, portfolio review...* I closed my laptop, took a breath, and prayed, "Lord, You're going to have to help me with this one."

Every state in the U.S. has its own homeschool laws. Some simple, others more complex. In Alaska, you can homeschool with almost no reporting. In Pennsylvania, you'll submit a yearly affidavit and evaluation. Most states fall somewhere in between, asking families to notify local officials, keep attendance, or show samples of work.

For beginners, here's what helps:

1. **Start by learning your state's rules.** The Home School Legal Defense Association (HSLDA.org) has a plain-language guide for every state. Read it once, then read it again with a notebook.

2. **Keep good records.** I have a binder for each child. Inside are sample assignments, reading lists, and a simple attendance chart. It takes me fifteen minutes a week and saves me hours of panic later.

3. **Choose an assessment plan early.** Some states require annual testing, others accept a teacher review or portfolio. Pick what fits your child's learning style.

When I worried about doing something wrong, a veteran homeschool mom gave me advice that stuck: *"Be honest, be organized, and be calm. You're not hiding anything, you're educating your kids."*

Legal clarity gives peace of mind, but it also represents something bigger, the recognition that parents are trusted to direct their children's education. The road here wasn't easy. In the 1980s, parents fought court battles to secure that freedom. By 1993, homeschooling was legal in all fifty states.

Globally, the picture varies. Some countries, like Canada, Australia, and the U.K., openly allow homeschooling. Others restrict or ban it. In Germany, for instance, parents can face fines for teaching children outside the state system. Those contrasts remind me how precious our freedom to homeschool truly is.

I keep one guiding principle at the center: **teach openly and honestly.** We invite accountability because it builds credibility. When my husband and I submit our yearly notice, it's not an act of fear it's stewardship. We're saying, "We're here, we're responsible, and we're doing this with integrity."

Faith shapes how I approach it too. Romans 13:1 tells us to respect governing authorities, and I believe that includes doing our homeschool paperwork diligently. We can model for our children how to follow rules without losing joy.

If legal details ever feel overwhelming, remember that you're part of a long line of parents who fought for this right so you could freely teach your children at home. When I file our notice each year now, I whisper a quick prayer of gratitude for the families who paved the way and for the quiet, everyday freedom to learn together.

homeschooling: the benefits beyond academics

One morning, my ten-year-old son sat at the table balancing a ruler, a pencil, and a cookie. "If I eat half," he said, "is that fifty percent?" He grinned like a mad scientist. That's when I realized: learning was happening, even with crumbs on the math workbook.

Homeschooling isn't only about academics. It shapes family life, character, and creativity in ways no test score can measure.

1. Customized learning.

In a homeschool, lessons fit the child, not the other way around. My oldest daughter loves art. So when we studied history, we painted scenes from ancient Egypt and built a cardboard Nile. My son, on the other hand, learns best through motion, so we use basketball shots to practice multiplication. Tailoring education like this builds confidence.

The National Home Education Research Institute found that homeschooled students consistently score 15–30 percentile points above public-school averages on standardized tests, regardless of parents' education level. But beyond the numbers, they often report greater satisfaction and curiosity in learning.

2. Family connection.

When you spend your days learning together, small moments accumulate into lifelong memories. Reading aloud on the couch, impromptu science experiments, kitchen-table devotions these aren't extras; they're the core. We've laughed over exploding baking soda volcanoes, argued (lovingly) over grammar, and cried through *The Hiding Place*. Each memory weaves another stitch in the family fabric.

3. Life skills.

School days double as preparation for life. My teens plan meals for home economics, calculate costs for budgeting, and learn how to manage time when they babysit or work part-time. The home becomes a real-world lab for responsibility and teamwork.

4. Faith and character.

We start mornings with Scripture and prayer, not because we're perfect, but because it centers our hearts. When conflicts erupt, usually around who gets the last pencil, I remind myself that this is where patience, forgiveness, and humility are taught best: in real life, at home, between siblings.

5. Freedom and pace.

Homeschooling lets us follow our natural rhythms. We can finish lessons early and take a picnic to the park or stretch a unit study for weeks if interest blooms. We take field trips on quiet weekdays when museums are empty. And when life throws curveballs, a new baby, a sick grandparent, we adjust without guilt.

I've often thought of homeschooling as a long road trip. The map is yours, but God handles the terrain. You may hit potholes, detours, or unexpected beauty, but you're still moving toward the same destination: raising children who love to learn, love others, and love the Lord.

And yes, on some days you'll question everything. You'll wonder if you're doing enough or if they're learning what they should. But when you catch your kids explaining photosynthesis to their little sister using broccoli and a flashlight, you'll know you're doing something right.

Homeschooling gives families the rare chance to live, learn, and grow side by side. It's messy, loud, beautiful and it works.

all TOO common myths

When we first started homeschooling, I braced myself for the questions. At family gatherings, someone always asked with a polite smile, "But what about socialization?" One uncle joked, "So... are you going to make little house uniforms too?" I laughed, but later that night, while folding laundry, I whispered to my husband, "What if they're right? What if our kids really do turn out weird?"

That's the thing about homeschooling myths, they sound believable until you actually live this life.

The "socialization" myth

The truth? Our kids have more social interaction now than they did in traditional school. It just looks different. We meet twice a week with a local homeschool co-op. Tuesdays are for science labs; Thursdays for art, choir, and sometimes messy history reenactments. They've got sports through the city league, church youth group on Wednesdays, and impromptu neighborhood bike races nearly every afternoon.

Plus, think about what we've seen over the last 10-15 years. What kind of socialization do kids actually get at government schools? And is that what you want for your kids?

Homeschooling doesn't lead to isolation, unless you already live an isolated life

A 2020 study from the *Journal of School Choice* found that homeschooled students are often more socially engaged across age groups than their public-school peers. They spend more time interacting with adults, siblings, and children of different ages, mirroring real-world relationships.

My daughter's best friends include a 16-year-old budding graphic designer, a 12-year-old who raises chickens, and a 9-year-old who can recite *The Hobbit* by heart (kind of). That mix keeps them curious and kind.

But socialization doesn't just happen it's cultivated. And the homeschool community is thriving with opportunities: park meetups, youth theater, debate clubs, church events, and service projects. When people ask, I usually smile and say, "Don't worry. They talk plenty."

The "academic rigor" myth

Another myth says homeschoolers fall behind. Honestly, that one scared me the most. I didn't want my kids to miss something "important." But the first year proved otherwise. Freed from test-prep drills and one-size-fits-all pacing, we covered more material, not less. We went deep instead of fast.

When we studied ecosystems, the kids built terrariums, charted rainfall, and kept bug journals. My son presented his findings (complete with a live beetle guest) at co-op, speaking with a confidence I'd never seen before. That's not falling behind, that's thriving.

Nationwide testing data from the National Home Education Research Institute shows that homeschoolers score 15–30 percentile points higher on standardized tests, regardless of parents' education level or income. The difference isn't magic; it's time and attention.

The "parent qualifications" myth

I'm not a certified teacher. I have a bachelor's degree in communications, a love for books, and a deep need for coffee. But that doesn't disqualify me. Homeschooling isn't about mastering every subject, it's about being willing to learn alongside your kids. When we hit algebra, we hired a tutor. For biology, we joined a lab co-op. The internet opened doors to experts I'd never meet otherwise.

The myth that you must be a professional to teach your child misses the point. God equips those He calls. If you feel led to homeschool, He'll meet you in the gaps, with patience, resources, and unexpected help.

The "time and money" myth

Yes, homeschooling takes time. But not every waking minute. We finish formal lessons by early afternoon most days. That leaves space for chores, projects, and play. Financially, we spend less than most people expect. Our biggest costs are curriculum and field trips. But free resources abound, library books, YouTube tutorials, Khan Academy, and local museums. Many homeschoolers spend between $300–$800 per child per year, far less than private school tuition.

When people say, "I could never afford that," I tell them it's less about money and more about mindset. You trade some convenience for connection.

Faith reflection

The longer I homeschool, the more I see these myths for what they are: fear wearing logic's disguise. Fear of failure, of isolation, of doing it "wrong." But 2 Timothy 1:7 reminds me, *"For God has not given us a spirit of fear, but of power and of love and of a sound mind."* If He's called you to this, He's already given you what you need.

One evening last fall, my husband asked our ten-year-old, "What's your favorite part of homeschool?" He shrugged. "You guys," he said. "I like being with you." That's the kind of "socialization" I never want to lose.

philosophies from montessori to classical & more

I used to think there was one "right way" to homeschool, some perfect philosophy that would unlock harmony and academic bliss. Then I discovered the truth: homeschooling philosophies are like parenting styles. You borrow what fits, toss what doesn't, and adjust as your kids grow.

One fall evening, I found myself on the couch surrounded by books, *The Well-Trained Mind, Charlotte Mason Companion, Montessori from the Start,* and a cup of rapidly cooling tea. My husband walked by and asked, "Are we starting a school or a library?" I laughed. "Just trying to figure out who we are."

That night, I realized that philosophies aren't rules, they're tools. They give structure to our values and show us how kids learn best.

The Montessori method

Developed by Dr. Maria Montessori in the early 1900s, this approach focuses on independence, sensory exploration, and hands-on learning. Kids move freely between activities, learning practical skills alongside academic ones.

In our home, we use Montessori ideas mostly with the younger kids. The four-year-old pours her own juice with a small glass pitcher. She folds towels (crookedly) and sweeps with a tiny broom. We keep low shelves with baskets labeled "Letters," "Math," and "Art." She learns by touching, doing, and observing.

Montessori taught me that even small children are capable when given responsibility. It's a living parable of stewardship: God entrusts us with much, and we learn through doing.

The Charlotte Mason philosophy

Charlotte Mason, a British educator from the late 1800s, believed education is "an atmosphere, a discipline, a life." That phrase lives on sticky notes all over my house. She emphasized *living books*, well-written stories instead of dry textbooks, short lessons, and daily time in nature.

We follow her lead. Each morning we read from Scripture, a biography, or a historical novel. Then we go outside, no matter the season. Some of our best lessons have happened during muddy spring hikes or while sketching leaves in the backyard.

This approach aligns with how faith and learning intertwine. When you notice creation closely, you can't help but see the Creator. Psalm 19:1 says, *"The heavens declare the glory of God; the skies proclaim the work of his hands."*

The classical method

The classical philosophy, rooted in ancient Greece and the Middle Ages, structures learning in three stages called the trivium: grammar (knowledge), logic (understanding), and rhetoric (communication).My older kids thrive here. The grammar stage fills their minds with facts through repetition and memorization. The logic stage, typically middle school, teaches them to ask "why." And the rhetoric stage, the high school years, helps them express and defend ideas clearly.

When we studied the American Revolution, my daughter memorized key dates (grammar), debated whether rebellion was justified (logic), and wrote a persuasive essay from Abigail Adams's point of view (rhetoric). I realized this approach doesn't just teach history, it builds thinkers.

The eclectic blend

Of course, our real homeschool doesn't fit neatly into any single model. We're a patchwork quilt of methods. Mornings start with Charlotte Mason-style readings. Afternoons might follow classical logic or spontaneous unschooling projects, like the day my son turned the driveway into an "aquatic erosion experiment" with the hose.

That flexibility keeps things alive. Education becomes less about a system and more about formation, the shaping of heart and mind. Proverbs 22:6 reminds us, *"Train up a child in the way he should go."* That "way" might look a little different for every child.

Finding your fit

If you're just starting, don't feel pressured to declare your philosophy right away. Try a few styles. Visit co-ops. Borrow curriculum from a friend. Over time, you'll find what works for your children, and for you.

When moms ask which philosophy I "believe in," I smile and say, "The one that keeps peace in our house." That's the truth. A peaceful home is fertile ground for learning.

Homeschooling philosophies aren't cages; they're compass points. They help you orient yourself when the journey feels long. And when in doubt, remember: your relationship with your children is the curriculum that matters most.

designing your curriculum

If I could go back to our first homeschool year, I'd tell myself one thing: *Jennifer, the curriculum is your servant, not your master.*

Back then, I thought the "perfect curriculum" existed somewhere out there, maybe hidden inside a glossy catalog or a blog post written by a mom who owned a laminator and a label maker. I spent weeks researching, comparing reviews, and building color-coded spreadsheets. My printer practically smoked.

Then, halfway through our first semester, I realized something: the curriculum wasn't working, at least not for *us.* My oldest daughter dreaded her reading workbook. My son, who loved numbers, found his math program confusing. The four-year-old ate half her flashcards. I sat at the table one night surrounded by papers, tears welling up, and said to my husband, "I think I bought a shelf of guilt."

That's when it clicked. Homeschooling isn't about buying the perfect plan; it's about **building** one.

Step 1: start with your child, not the catalog

The most powerful curriculum begins with observation, not ordering. Watch what lights your child up. What do they talk about at dinner? What do they choose during free time? Those are clues to how they learn best.

One of my daughters learns through stories, if you hand her a novel about the American Revolution, she'll remember every detail. My son? He needs to touch and build. We made timelines out of painter's tape and used LEGO bricks to study multiplication arrays.

Homeschooling gives you permission to teach that way, to match your lessons to the child God uniquely designed.

Step 2: choose tools that fit your season

In education circles, people love to debate curriculum brands, but here's the secret most veteran homeschool moms know: **the best curriculum is the one you'll actually use.**

There are seasons when structure helps: workbooks, checklists, daily plans. Then there are seasons when open-ended unit studies bring joy back into learning. In 2022, when I had a toddler and a newborn, I used pre-planned lesson kits because I simply didn't have the energy to create anything from scratch. The following year, when life slowed down, we switched to a literature-based curriculum that allowed for long read- alouds and nature journaling.

Flexibility isn't failure, it's wisdom. Ecclesiastes 3 reminds us, *"There is a time for everything, and a season for every activity under the heavens."* That includes your homeschool seasons too.

Step 3: build rhythm, not rigidity

I learned quickly that I don't need a bell schedule. We keep a rhythm instead, a predictable flow with room for grace.

Our mornings start with "morning time," where all the kids gather for Scripture, read-alouds, and a short prayer. Then we branch off into math, writing, and reading. By lunchtime, we're often surrounded by notebooks and snack crumbs. After lunch is for experiments, art, or outdoor exploration.

The goal isn't perfect structure, it's peaceful consistency. We can miss a day without panic because our rhythm always leads us back home.

Step 4: evaluate gently and adjust often

Every six weeks, I take an evening to look through our work, what's finished, what's stuck, what's thriving. I ask each child, "What's your favorite subject right now? What's frustrating you?" Their answers tell me more than any test.

When something consistently causes stress, we pivot. Once, I replaced a dull grammar program with creative writing prompts, and suddenly my reluctant writer was crafting stories about pirate hamsters.

Evaluation isn't judgment, it's stewardship. You're tending souls, not running a factory.

Homeschool curriculum design is an act of creativity and love. It's building a learning world around your children, piece by piece. Sometimes it looks like paint-splattered notebooks and half-finished projects. Sometimes it's a quiet morning where everyone's focused, the coffee's still warm, and you think, *Maybe I really can do this.*

And when doubt creeps in, I remind myself of this truth: God didn't choose the "perfect teacher" for my kids, He chose **me.**

your child's learning style

Last winter, during a spelling lesson, my son slumped over the table and groaned, "Mom, my brain doesn't work that way!"

It was one of those moments every homeschool parent has, the flash of frustration that turns into revelation. He wasn't being dramatic; he was being honest. The way I was teaching didn't fit the way he learned.

That night, I sat on the couch scrolling through articles about "learning styles." I realized what every seasoned homeschool mom eventually learns: not all kids learn the same way, and that's okay.

The visual learner

Visual learners absorb information through images, charts, and written words. One of my daughters falls in this camp. She color-codes everything. Her math notes look like a rainbow exploded, and she remembers it all.

To teach her, we use diagrams, illustrated books, and color markers for vocabulary. When we read about geography, she sketches maps. When we study anatomy, she draws cross-sections of the heart. Seeing the concept cements it in her memory.

The auditory learner

My middle daughter, however, could memorize an entire passage just by hearing it. She learns best when she can talk it out.

During history, she reads aloud to herself, narrating key points. During math, she explains the steps back to me while pacing the kitchen. When she's stuck, we talk through the problem, and halfway through her explanation, she suddenly grins and says, "Never mind, I got it."

Auditory learners thrive on rhythm, conversation, and music. We play classical tracks during writing time and set memory facts to songs. Faith memory verses come alive that way too, our house often sounds like a hymn rehearsal and a spelling bee collided.

The kinesthetic learner

Then there's my ten-year-old, our kinesthetic learner. If he can move, he can learn. I once caught him spelling words by bouncing a basketball, each letter a dribble. He learns fractions by slicing apples, history by building model forts, and spelling by writing words in sidewalk chalk.

Homeschooling gives him space to move. Traditional desks never suited him. So now we rotate: lessons at the table, the porch, or even on a blanket in the yard.

The blend and the blessing

Most kids are a mix. My younger ones bounce between visual and kinesthetic, while my oldest prefers silence and lists. The key is noticing what works. Observe, adapt, and give yourself grace.

God designed each child uniquely. Psalm 139 reminds us, *"You knit me together in my mother's womb."* Learning style is part of that divine design. Our job isn't to force them into a mold, it's to discover how they're wired and teach accordingly.

Encouragement for the weary teacher

Learning styles aren't boxes, they're clues. Use them to spark curiosity, not to limit growth.

If your visual learner loves diagrams, let her illustrate her Bible verse. If your auditory learner memorizes through song, make it a duet while folding laundry. If your kinesthetic learner can't sit still, turn math drills into hopscotch.

There's no "wrong" way to learn when the goal is understanding, not performance.

One evening, after a particularly chaotic day, I told my husband, "I feel like I'm juggling seven different schools." He smiled and said, "You are, but that's your ministry."

And he's right. Every child's uniqueness is a gift. Homeschooling lets us unwrap it slowly, lovingly, one subject, one season, one miracle at a time.

the heart behind homeschooling

When I look back on those early days, the messy schedules, the math tears, the laughter spilling out during read-alouds, I see a picture God was painting the whole time.

Homeschooling didn't just change how my children learn. It changed *me.* It slowed me down. It made me depend less on checklists and more on prayer. It reminded me that raising kids isn't about managing performance, it's about shaping hearts.

If you're standing at the start of your homeschool journey, maybe feeling unsure or overwhelmed, take courage. You don't need a perfect plan. You just need willingness. God multiplies that willingness into wisdom.

You're about to embark on one of the most refining, joyful, sanctifying adventures of your life. You'll teach math and grammar, but you'll also teach patience, forgiveness, faith, and wonder. You'll discover that the real curriculum is love lived out, day after day, lesson after lesson.

So take a deep breath. Clear the kitchen table. Gather your pencils, your coffee, and your courage. You're ready.

my story: pencils, pancakes, and permission Slips

When people hear I homeschool seven kids, they look at me like I'm climbing Everest barefoot. Some days it feels that way. Most days it feels like grace in a noisy kitchen.

We didn't decide in a boardroom with charts and pros-and-cons lists. We decided at the kitchen table, the way most of our important decisions are made—between a sippy cup, a cold cup of coffee, and a stack of mail I kept meaning to open. The baby was teething and gnawing on a silicone giraffe. Our ten-year-old had built a launch pad out of cereal boxes and was giving a speech about thrust, except his speech was mostly sound effects. The teens were both angry at their laptops for different reasons. I stood there, wooden spoon in one hand, and whispered toward the sink, "Lord, what would peace look like for us?"

The question lingered over the steam of oatmeal.

That night, when everyone had finally stopped lapping the hallway and the dishwasher was the only thing still humming, I told my husband, "I don't want to spend another year managing chaos we didn't create."

He wiped his hands on a dish towel, not looking surprised. "Then let's build the thing we wish existed," he said. "At home."

We didn't start with a manifesto. We started with an index card. On it we wrote our why and taped it inside the pantry door where only the cereal and I would see it every morning: *Home is sacred ground—connection before clocks.*

The next Monday I sharpened twelve pencils like little flags of hope and lined them in a row down the table. The baby swiped two immediately and crawled away, triumphant. I lit a candle—because if you can't control the noise, at least you can choose to make it smell like vanilla—and I said, "Okay, team. We're trying school at home."

Our fourth grader raised her hand earnestly. "Does that mean recess happens in our yard or the church playground?"

"Yes," I said. "Both."

The truth is, I had no idea what I was doing, and the larger truth is that parents have been teaching their children at home for as long as there have been homes. That thought became a thread I pulled and pulled. Long before bells and buses, children learned by shadowing adults, reading aloud by lamplight, measuring wood for shelves, reciting psalms while shelling peas. Somewhere along the way—whistles, clocks, tidy rows—home became something you returned to after learning, instead of where learning began. And then, slowly, it circled back. Not because a committee decreed it, but because ordinary families, just like ours, wanted to hold their kids closer to the fire that warms them.

I used to picture those early homeschoolers—the ones whose kids are grown now—as pioneers with denim jumpers and impossibly neat handwriting. Then I met one at co-op. She told me how, in the early nineties, she'd host chemistry at her dining table, then hide the glassware under a tablecloth before guests arrived. "I got tired of hiding what we were proud of," she said. "Eventually the neighbors started asking to come over for labs." We laughed. "We were just parents, not rebels," she added, and I tucked that sentence in my pocket like a prayer.

The second Tuesday of our first week, I sat at the counter with a form open on the laptop: *Intent to Homeschool.* The baby was chewing the eraser off a pencil. The middle kids were choreographing a recess routine that involved a broom and a beach towel. The teens were halfway through a debate about whether a thesis could be funny. I stared at the form, breathed in vanilla and oatmeal, and said out loud, as if my own voice could steady me, "Okay, Jennifer. You're doing this."

Paperwork felt scarier than phonics, to be honest. Legal language is not written by people who have toddlers climbing them like a jungle gym. I found HSLDA's plain-English guide, read it twice, printed a copy, and wrote in the margin: *Breathe. Be honest, be organized, be calm.* A friend's advice from church. I kept records the way I keep grocery lists—simply, faithfully, with smeared pen and grace for smudges. We made a binder for each child. Inside: a reading log with cocoa stains, a math page that used to feel impossible, a poem copied out in curly handwriting, a photo of a volcano we made in the driveway that erupted too enthusiastically and baptized the mailbox.

When I pressed "submit," I whispered, "Thank You—for the parents who fought the boring battles so we can do the beautiful work." Filing wasn't fear for me; it felt like stewardship. We were saying, "We'll do this in the light. Come see." And later, when the state reminder arrived to file again next year, the task felt less like obligation and more like gratitude, like leaving the porch light on for friends.

The day after we filed, I tried to teach a spelling lesson from a workbook I'd chosen for its cheery fonts. My ten-year-old slumped so far over the table he looked like a melting snowman. "Mom," he groaned, the word a whole paragraph of despair, "my brain doesn't work that way."

It was one of those sharp little moments that rearrange furniture in your head. He wasn't being dramatic; he was being honest. I had shoved him into a pair of shoes that didn't fit and then wondered why he didn't want to run. That night, after everyone slept and the house made its nighttime clicks and sighs, I read about learning styles with a pen in my hand. Visual. Auditory. Kinesthetic. I thought about our daughter who color-codes her existence and remembers the entire plot of anything we've ever read if she's allowed to sketch it. I thought about another who can memorize a page just by hearing it. And I thought about our son—my moving encyclopedia—who learns best when his sneakers are scuffed. I made a quiet promise to each of them: *I will learn how you learn.*

The next morning, I put the spelling workbook back on the shelf and pulled out sidewalk chalk. "Spelling bee," I said, pointing to the driveway. He wrote his word the size of a bicycle and added flames. We sang our history timeline while unloading the dishwasher. We practiced math facts with the basketball hoop: "Six times seven," I called. "Forty-two!" he yelled, swish. Meanwhile, his sister read me a page from a biography while sketching the subject's eyebrows with intense focus. The baby napped for exactly nineteen minutes, woke up like a rooster, and we called that a good start.

We tried on philosophies like sweaters to see which ones fit and which ones made us itch. I stacked a pile of books beside the couch one evening—Charlotte Mason, Classical

Conversations resources, Montessori guides, a blog post about unschooling Fridays—and my husband squinted at the pile. "Are we starting a school or a library?" he asked.

"Both," I said. "Maybe."

We found our blend the way you find your kitchen's favorite mug: you just keep reaching for it. Mornings became our Charlotte Masonish time—Scripture, a hymn, a living book read with someone always eating an apple too loudly, and a nature walk even when nature looked like ten minutes around the block with coats half-zipped. The middle stretch leaned classical—memory work, logic puzzles, an argument about whether a thesis statement can, in fact, be sassy (jury's still out). And Fridays we loosened the laces—unschooling, more or less. Build the bird house, bake the bread, code the little game, dig the hole you're sure will reach Australia. (It did not. But the hole was magnificent.)

We called it a rhythm, not a schedule. I kept a thrift-store bell on the shelf and rang it when we shifted lanes. The bell didn't make us efficient; it made us smile. Morning time. Math sprints. Writing. Lunch. Loop subjects in the afternoon that waited politely if life ran late—history, science, art, music. When the day went sideways—and it did, spectacularly, on the regular—we practiced saying, "Enough for today." We tidied to music and called the work complete. On truly bonkers days, I declared a Grace Day and made pancakes for dinner. Syrup is its own liturgy.

The first time someone asked about socialization, we were at a birthday party. A nice aunt, warm smile, genuine curiosity. "But... what about friends?" she asked, eyes flicking toward my kids playing musical chairs with a pack of cousins and two toddlers who refused to sit at all.

I took a breath and decided to tell the truth without getting defensive. "We have a co-op on Tuesdays for labs," I said. "On Thursdays, there's choir and ridiculous art projects I wouldn't attempt at home. City-league basketball. Youth group on Wednesdays. Board games with the neighbors. And a surprising number of conversations with older adults who teach them how to listen well."

She nodded slowly. "So... regular life."

"Exactly," I smiled. "Just... more of it together."

That was a gift I didn't anticipate—the way our kids' worlds widened and deepened at the same time. The seven-year-old's best friends span three grades and two zip codes. The teen asked an eighty-three-year-old at church how she bakes her bread, and now we have a standing monthly lesson called "Flour and Stories." Socialization stops sounding like a concern when you realize what you've been practicing is community.

It wasn't all watercolor journals and sourdough, of course. Mid-October I realized I had bought a shelf of guilt. The reading workbook made one child wilt. The math program made another suspicious of numbers. I had a toddler with an uncanny ability to locate and eat flashcards. One night I sat among the castle of curriculum boxes with tears in my eyes and told my husband, "I think I chose what looked good in a catalog, not what would work in our Tuesday."

He handed me a tissue and, with a gentleness I needed, said, "Then let's change what doesn't fit."

It felt like cheating at first. Isn't the virtuous thing to finish what you started? But the more I watched my children, the more I learned: curriculum is a servant, not a master. We swapped the reading program for novels and narration. We traded the confusing math for a clear, hands-on approach. We kept the parts that were working and gave away what wasn't. The next week, my reluctant reader read to the four-year-old on the couch while the toddler napped and the house went oddly quiet, like the walls were listening.

We kept gentle records. Once a month we hosted Celebration Tea. Each kid brought one thing: a sentence copied carefully, a sketch from the park, a math page they'd battled and won, a paragraph about a frog. I snapped a photo of each and typed a one-line note with the date. That shoebox of photos and the little Google Doc grew into evidence of something larger than productivity. It was faithfulness on paper.

What surprised me most that first year was how the learning we worried about happened in the cracks we didn't plan. My son asked if eating half a cookie was fifty percent. We called it math with crumbs. A hike turned into botany because the girls discovered a field guide in the glove compartment. A documentary during quiet time became a dinner table debate about whether a character's choices were brave or foolish. The teens started helping the younger ones because I couldn't be everywhere at once; their teaching cemented their learning. The house felt like a lived-in university—noisy, sometimes sticky, but earnest.

One Saturday we built a paper timeline down the hallway with painter's tape and sticky notes. The kids stuck drawings to the dates while my husband flipped pancakes. I slid a plate under my teen's nose and asked, "Would you trade places with anyone on this wall?"

She tapped a year and thought hard. "Maybe. But I think I like having a washing machine."

"Reasonable," I said. Perspective is a unit study too.

At some point in November, a neighbor asked, "But are they keeping up?" I knew what she meant. Are you covering enough? Will they be okay in the grand march of checklists?

"We go deep instead of fast," I told her. "When we studied ecosystems, they built terrariums, charted rainfall, and kept bug journals. My son presented his findings at co-op with a very alive beetle guest and the proudest grin I've ever seen." She smiled. "That sounds like keeping up," she said. I nodded, surprised by the steadiness in my voice. "It does."

And then there was the myth about time. People assumed we did school until dusk. The truth: most days our formal lessons wrapped by early afternoon. The rest of the day dissolved into chores, side projects, and the kind of play that looks lazy until you realize it's wiring the brain for creativity. It required a trade—less convenience, more connection. But it gave us back our family life, and I will make that trade every time.

We met the law with a clear conscience. We sent in the notices, kept the attendance (with generous rounding and honest notes—"sick"—"field trip to the library"—"life skills: baked bread and negotiated whose turn it was to unload the dishwasher"). When one of the kids asked why we had to fill out a form at all, I told her a simple truth: "Because we live with people, not just ourselves. And because other parents stood in meetings and wrote letters so we could do this freely. We say thank you by doing the boring parts on time." She nodded like that made sense and went back to drawing a beetle with an alarming number of legs.

Our co-op became a warm spine to the week. Twenty families, a borrowed church building, a whiteboard that always squeaked. There was a dad who ran small engine repair in the parking lot, a mom who did Shakespeare with pool noodles, another who straightened my grammar plan like a kind librarian. The kids did messy labs I wouldn't attempt at home (elephant toothpaste remains on my conscience) and presentations that taught them how to look a room in the eye. We planned a service day at the nursing home; the kids sang "Great Is Thy Faithfulness," and an older gentleman cried into his handkerchief. He told my son afterward, "It's good to see young people who look up when they talk." Socialization, it turns out, looks a lot like belonging.

My favorite moments were small ones that felt like God tapping my shoulder. The morning a spelling lesson dissolved in tears over a pencil, I heard the nudge: pause. We closed the book, moved to the couch. "We can do work with grumpy hearts," I said quietly, "or we can do the harder thing—make it right." We prayed a one-sentence prayer: "Jesus, help us love." Ten minutes later, the same pencil was shared like a peace treaty. The math took longer, but the lesson went deeper. Character isn't extra credit; it's the curriculum.

We learned to call a thing "enough." We learned to say, "Try this," and then, just as importantly, "This isn't working—let's pivot." We learned to respect our seasons—tight planning the year the baby came, more meandering the year after when we all needed a longer exhale. Ecclesiastes kept visiting our kitchen: *a time to plant and a time to uproot; a time to keep and a time to throw away; a time to be silent and a time to speak.* (Also: a time to eat pancakes for dinner because the dishwasher died and the dog threw up a sock.)

By spring, if you'd walked into our house at 9:07 a.m., you would have found a particular liturgy: candle lit, a hymn sung too low by morning voices, a psalm read with sticky fingers, a poem about geese, someone on the floor building a castle and insisting it was, in fact, "related to history." You would have found me at the head of the table, not as a perfect teacher, but as a devoted one, cheeks smudged with pencil from wiping them with the back of my hand, heart steadier than it had been in a long time. You would have heard laughter, bickering, apology, the bell, the scrape of chairs, the drone of a pencil sharpener that hates us, and in the middle of it—learning. Real learning. The kind that sticks because it's attached to people who love you.

One evening, as the sun slid through the slats and turned our crumbs to gold dust, my husband asked our son, "What's your favorite part of homeschool?"

He shrugged and tried to look casual. "You guys," he said finally, then ducked his head. "I like being with you."

I looked at the pantry door where our index card still hung. *Connection before clocks.* The card is splattered with who-knows-what now, corners curling, words still true.

Friend, if you're standing at the edge of all this, heart thudding, wondering if you are enough, hear me: you aren't behind. Today counts because you showed up with love. You don't have to pick the perfect method on a Tuesday or master the legalese before lunch. Start with your why. File the paper with a calm heart. Light a candle. Read one good page. Eat math if it helps. Ask forgiveness at noon and begin again at twelve-oh-eight.

We turned our house into a school, yes. But more than that, we turned our days into a long conversation—with God, with each other, with the world He made. Homeschooling didn't make us perfect; it made us present. And that, it turns out, is the secret sauce. Not a laminated chart. Not a spreadsheet. Presence.

Tomorrow morning I'll set out pencils like small promises. Someone will lose one immediately. Someone will ask how rockets work at the exact moment I'm trying to teach long division. We'll file a paper when it's due and show our work without fear. We'll argue, apologize, and eat a fraction of a cookie while discussing percentages. And at 11:47, I'll put my hand on the bell, look around the table, and say the words that keep our house soft: "That's enough for today."

Not perfect, but faithful. That's enough for today.

laying the groundwork for success

preparation is key

The night before our first official homeschool day, I laid out notebooks, sharpened pencils, and fresh crayons. I even lit a candle, hoping it would make the kitchen feel less like a cafeteria and more like a cozy one-room schoolhouse.

Then the baby woke up twice. The printer jammed. The candle dripped wax all over my "first day" planner.

By 9 a.m., I'd learned my first lesson: preparation doesn't mean perfection.

Homeschooling doesn't begin with curriculum, it begins with *heart*. It's about preparing your home, your time, and your spirit for a journey that will test and bless you in equal measure.

When I meet new homeschool moms, they often ask, "What curriculum should I buy first?" I always answer, "Patience. Buy patience first."

You don't need everything figured out, but you do need to lay a foundation that can hold the weight of real life, because homeschooling will test that foundation.

For me, that foundation had three layers: **calling, clarity, and courage.**

Calling. I started homeschooling out of conviction, not convenience. COVID cracked open my faith in the public system, but prayer sealed my decision. I felt God nudge my heart: *Bring them home.* That quiet whisper carried me through days when I wanted to quit.

Clarity. Knowing *why* you homeschool will anchor you when emotions rise. Maybe it's faith, family closeness, special needs, or academic flexibility. Write that reason down and post it somewhere visible. Mine's taped inside my kitchen cabinet: "Because God called me to shepherd their hearts."

Courage. You won't feel ready. None of us did. But you're not walking into this alone. God fills the gaps. Every veteran homeschool mom will tell you, the first year teaches *you* as much as it teaches your kids.

Preparation doesn't guarantee smooth sailing, but it gives you tools to steady the ship when storms come. Proverbs 24:3 reminds us, *"By wisdom a house is built, and through understanding it is established."*

physical space, time, and mindset

I used to think I needed a Pinterest-perfect classroom, chalkboard walls, alphabet garlands, matching desks. Then reality set in: seven kids, one dining room table, and a toddler who thought crayons were snacks.

So we adapted. Our "schoolroom" became the kitchen table, the couch, the front porch, and sometimes the trunk of the van during soccer practice. Learning, I realized, doesn't depend on fancy spaces, it depends on intention.

Physical space

Start with what you have. A bookshelf for materials, a cabinet for supplies, and a consistent surface for writing are all you truly need. Some families thrive with a dedicated schoolroom; others prefer spreading out across the home.

We keep a simple basket system: one for morning time books, one for math, one for creative projects. On Fridays, we tidy everything back into its place, a small act that keeps chaos from swallowing the week.

Remember: kids don't need a classroom; they need a place where curiosity feels welcome.

Time

Next comes the question every new homeschooler wrestles with: *How do I fit this in?*

Here's the good news, homeschooling doesn't have to mimic a six-hour school day. A 2021 HSLDA survey found that most families spend between two and four focused hours per day on formal academics, with the rest devoted to reading, play, chores, and exploration.

Our rhythm looks like this:

- **Morning (9–12):** Group learning and core subjects.

- **Afternoon (1–3):** Projects, nature time, or co-op classes.

- **Evening:** Reading aloud or music practice.

It's not rigid; it's repeatable. Some days we're done by noon, others stretch longer. The key is balance, not busyness.

When schedules unravel, and they will, I remind myself that consistency over time matters more than perfection today.

Mindset

Homeschooling tests your mindset as much as your patience. The biggest shift is this: **you're not replicating school, you're reimagining education.**

Give yourself permission to learn alongside your children. Laugh at the flops. Start over when needed. You'll have messy days and miraculous ones, sometimes back-to-back.

One morning, after a chaotic math lesson that ended in tears (mine), I stepped outside, closed my eyes, and prayed, "Lord, help me see them the way You do." That small prayer changed my tone for the rest of the day.

Mindset shapes atmosphere. When you lead with grace, your home becomes a place where mistakes are part of learning, not reasons for shame.

what you need to get started

When I first began homeschooling, I thought I needed *everything*. The glossy catalogs made it look like success required an entire warehouse: specialized pencils, magnetic timelines, scented markers, color-coded bins, and about six different math programs.

What I actually needed was far simpler, and far more human.

Here's what truly matters when gathering resources:

1. A plan, not a pile

Start with your goals. What do you want your children to learn this semester? Maybe it's multiplication, reading fluency, or a better attitude during chores (that counts too).

Once you know your goals, choose resources that align with them. You don't need the most expensive or popular options, just materials that fit your family's rhythm.

2. Books, lots of them

Books are the backbone of homeschooling. Keep a steady rotation of picture books, biographies, historical fiction, and devotionals. We keep a "family basket" by the couch and refresh it weekly from the library.

Reading aloud is our favorite part of the day. It builds vocabulary, connection, and memory all at once. Some of our best discussions have started with a simple question: "What do you think that character should have done?"

3. Basic supplies that invite creativity

Here's my must-have list: pencils, paper, a globe, glue sticks, markers, a laptop with internet access, and curiosity. Everything else is optional.

The best experiments often come from what's already in the kitchen. Once, my kids learned about buoyancy by floating random household items in the bathtub. Educational *and* entertaining, until someone dropped my phone in the water. (It survived.)

4. Community and support

No curriculum can replace community. Find a homeschool group or co-op near you. These networks share lesson plans, field trip ideas, and sometimes much-needed empathy.

When I joined our first co-op, I walked in nervously, clutching a notebook. Another mom smiled and said, "You're new, right? Don't worry, we all started scared." I nearly cried right there in the church basement. Those women became my lifeline.

The Bible reminds us in Ecclesiastes 4:9, *"Two are better than one, because they have a good return for their labor."* Homeschooling is richer when done in community.

create a supportive group

When I first decided to homeschool, I felt like I was standing on an island with a handful of library books and a whole lot of questions. My husband was supportive, but even he joked, "You're going to need a teacher's lounge."

He was right, I just didn't know what that looked like yet.

It wasn't until a friend from church invited me to a local homeschool co-op that I realized how vital community would become. The first morning, I carried a diaper bag, two notebooks, and enough snacks to feed an army. I walked in nervous but left encouraged. I had found my people.

Homeschooling may happen at home, but it doesn't happen *alone*.

Finding your people

Your support network might start small, a friend from church, a local Facebook group, or a library story hour. Many communities host park days, field trips, and co-ops. You don't have to join everything; find one or two that fit your family's rhythm.

Co-ops are especially valuable. They can be as simple as a few families trading teaching duties, or as organized as a full-day program with classes and electives. Our co-op meets twice a week in a church basement. Parents rotate teaching subjects, science, writing, art, and everyone chips in for supplies. My kids love it, and I get to talk with other moms who truly understand this life.

When you're new, it can feel intimidating. You'll meet families who've been home-schooling for years, who seem to have everything figured out. But here's the secret: *they're still learning too.* The beauty of community is that everyone brings something different, experience, ideas, encouragement.

Why community matters

A 2023 NHERI survey found that 78% of homeschooling parents reported lower stress and higher consistency when they were part of a regular support network. It's not just about academics; it's emotional sustainability.

When we hit a wall, say, the math curriculum meltdown of March, I text a friend who's been there. Her response is always the same: "Deep breath. Take a walk. Try again tomorrow." That kind of encouragement is worth more than any workbook.

Faith and friendship

God designed us for connection. Galatians 6:2 reminds us, *"Carry each other's burdens, and in this way you will fulfill the law of Christ."*

Homeschooling community isn't just about shared lesson plans; it's shared lives, prayers for sick kids, meals after new babies, laughter during park days, and the reassur-ance that we're not alone in this calling.

So reach out. Send that message. Show up to that first co-op meeting even if you're nervous. The friendships you build will become the backbone of your homeschool jour-ney.

having realistic expectations

The summer before our first homeschool year, I made a list that could rival NASA's launch checklist.

Teach all subjects with excellence. Keep the house clean. Bake bread weekly. No screen time before 3 p.m. Start piano lessons.

By October, I had crossed off one thing: "Buy bread instead."

It took me time to learn that realistic goals don't shrink dreams, they make them sustainable.

The homeschool year is a marathon, not a sprint

The first step is recognizing that this is a long game. You don't have to master everything by December. Start with two or three priorities per child. Maybe your third grader needs to gain confidence in reading. Maybe your high schooler needs structure in time management. Focus there.

We now set **quarterly goals** instead of yearlong ones. It keeps expectations flexible and celebrations frequent. I write them on sticky notes and post them on the fridge: "Learn all multiplication tables." "Finish our science project." "Read one classic novel as a family."

Measuring progress without pressure

In traditional school, progress often means grades and report cards. In homeschooling, it's more nuanced. You'll see progress in how your child approaches a challenge, not just whether they "get it right."

Last year, my daughter struggled through a tough math unit. I was ready to scrap the program, but then she said, "Mom, can I try one more time before you change it?" That persistence was the real victory.

Homeschooling gives you freedom to evaluate growth holistically, academically, emotionally, spiritually. Keep a journal or portfolio of those moments. They'll remind you how far you've come when doubt creeps in.

Grace over grind

The enemy of joy in homeschooling is comparison. It steals peace faster than a toddler with an open glue stick.

When you see that mom online whose kids are diagramming Latin sentences while yours are eating cereal during spelling, remember: you're seeing her highlight reel, not her Tuesday meltdown.

The only standard that matters is faithfulness, to your family, your season, and God's direction. Proverbs 16:3 says, *"Commit to the Lord whatever you do, and He will establish your plans."*

If your day ends with kids who felt loved and learned something new, that's success.

developing your homeschooling philosophy

Every homeschool has a heartbeat, a "why" that shapes its rhythm. Finding that heartbeat turns daily lessons into purpose.

When I started, I borrowed other people's philosophies: Charlotte Mason, Classical Conversations, even something called "Wild + Free" that involved a lot of nature walks and bare feet. (We lasted two weeks before the mosquitoes won.)

Eventually, through trial and prayer, our own philosophy emerged: *to cultivate wisdom, wonder, and faith.*

How to uncover your homeschool philosophy

Ask yourself a few grounding questions:

- What matters most to me in education?

- What do I want my children to remember about learning at home?

- What kind of adults am I trying to raise?

Your answers become the compass for decisions, curriculum, schedule, priorities.

For example, if your core value is *character*, you might emphasize service projects and Bible study. If it's *creativity*, you might structure your days around exploration and art. There's no wrong answer when it's intentional.

Writing it down

I encourage every family to write a short mission statement. Ours is taped inside our school cabinet:

"In our home, learning is worship. We seek knowledge with curiosity, practice truth with grace, and remember that wisdom begins with the fear of the Lord."

It's not fancy, but it centers us when the day feels scattered.

Faith reflection

In Deuteronomy 6, God instructs parents to teach His commandments diligently to their children, when they sit at home, when they walk along the road, when they lie down, and when they get up. That passage defines our homeschool philosophy better than any manual ever could.

Your philosophy is simply your *why* in action. Once you know it, every choice, curriculum, co-op, schedule, flows with greater peace.

flexibility

No one warned me how often plans would change.

One Tuesday, we had a perfect schedule: math, reading, nature study, lunch, then art. By 10:00 a.m., the baby had a fever, the Wi-Fi crashed, and the dog threw up on our history book.

I almost cried. Instead, we closed the books, made soup, and spent the afternoon reading *Little House in the Big Woods* out loud. That day taught me more about flexibility than any workshop ever could.

Flexibility is not failure

Homeschooling thrives when you learn to bend instead of break. Some days the lessons flow; other days, everyone, including you, needs a reset.

Rigid schedules can rob joy. But too much freedom can breed chaos. The sweet spot lies in **rhythm with grace**, predictable enough for progress, flexible enough for life.

When interruptions happen, I remind myself of Proverbs 19:21: *"Many are the plans in a person's heart, but it is the Lord's purpose that prevails."* God's lessons often hide in life's interruptions.

Practical ways to build flexibility

- **Plan "margin days."** Keep Fridays lighter for catch-up, errands, or rest.

- **Rotate focus subjects.** Deep-dive into one subject each week, history projects one week, science experiments the next.

- **Hold loosely to time.** If a lesson sparks excitement, ride that wave. A spontaneous conversation about the moon can teach more than a full worksheet ever will.

Flexibility models faith

Our kids watch how we respond when plans crumble. When they see us stay calm and gracious, we teach them trust. When they see us adjust with humor, we show them resilience.

Last fall, after a particularly messy week, my oldest daughter said, "Mom, you don't freak out anymore when stuff goes wrong." I smiled. "That's because I've had a lot of practice."

Homeschooling flexibility isn't just a skill, it's a spiritual discipline. It reminds us that control was never the goal; faithfulness is.

building confidence as a homeschooling mom

If I could bottle one thing for every new homeschool mom, it would be *confidence.* Not the loud, "I've got this" kind, but the quiet assurance that grows through experience and grace.

Confidence, for me, didn't come overnight. It came one day at a time, through tears, prayers, and tiny victories.

Remember where confidence comes from

Early on, I thought confidence meant mastering everything. Now I know it means trusting God to fill the gaps. Philippians 1:6 says, *"He who began a good work in you will carry it on to completion."*

Confidence blooms when you realize you're not alone. It's not about knowing all the answers, it's about believing you're called and equipped for this.

Celebrate small wins

Keep a "victory list." Ours includes everything from "finished our first novel" to "made it through a full week without anyone crying during math."

These tiny triumphs add up. They remind you that progress doesn't always look dramatic, it often looks like showing up again today.

Silence the comparison

Confidence shrinks when you compare your behind-the-scenes to someone else's highlight reel. God didn't give *them* your children, He gave them to *you*. Your family's path is custom-designed.

Whenever insecurity whispers, I remind myself of Ephesians 2:10: *"We are His workmanship, created in Christ Jesus for good works, which God prepared in advance for us to do."* That includes teaching our children.

The fruit of confidence

When a mother grows confident, her children flourish. They sense it. They rest in it. Confidence becomes contagious.

One evening, my daughter told me, "Mom, I like learning from you because you always believe I can figure it out." I blinked back tears. That's when I realized, the confidence I was building wasn't just for me; it was for them.

Homeschooling confidence isn't pride; it's peace. It's waking up each day and saying, "Lord, I don't have to be perfect, just present." And somehow, that's always enough.

the foundation beneath the journey

If Chapter 1 was about understanding *why* we homeschool, this chapter is about *how* to start with strength.

Preparation, space, support, and faith don't remove the chaos, they anchor you in it. The groundwork you lay now becomes the safety net for every hard day ahead.

Before moving into the daily rhythm of homeschooling, take a moment to thank God for the calling itself. It's holy work, raising minds and hearts at home.

Tomorrow, you'll plan lessons and sort supplies. But tonight, rest in this truth: the most important foundation isn't the curriculum or the schedule, it's your heart surrendered to His guidance.

You are not building a school. You're building a legacy.

my story: groundwork week

The night before our first official homeschool day, I lined up notebooks like obedient little soldiers and sharpened pencils until they looked like hope with erasers. I lit a candle because the internet told me ambiance matters, and if a flame could magically transform a Minnesota kitchen into a one-room schoolhouse, I was here for it. The printer, insulted by my optimism, jammed. The toddler woke twice to file formal complaints. The candle dripped a waxy constellation across my "First Day" planner and hardened there like a meteor shower.

By 9:03 a.m., the next morning, I had learned my first lesson: preparation is not perfection. It's faith with a to-do list.

"Okay," I said to the room, teens at half-mast, the ten-year-old testing the limits of gravity with a pencil behind his ear, the seven-year-old pairing markers like best friends, the four-year-old investigating whether crayons are food, the baby clapping smugly from her high chair. "We're doing school. At home. With grace."

"Do we still get recess?" the seven-year-old asked.

"Now you get two," I said, and made a mental note to Google "how much recess is too much."

That night, after the dishwasher hummed and the house exhaled, I sat with a mug and the quiet. The question that began our journey floated back like steam: *What would peace look like for us?* COVID had cracked something in me, the pace, the politics, the persistent hum of other people's alarms in our living room. But prayer had sealed the decision. *Bring them home,* God had whispered into the messy middle of my heart. So I did what I always do when something is bigger than me: I made a small card.

On an index card, in my crooked mom-script, I wrote three words, *Calling. Clarity. Courage.*, and taped it inside the pantry where only the cereal and I would see it every morning. Underneath, another line: *Home is sacred ground, connection before clocks.* The card winked at me when I reached for oatmeal. It steadied me when my plan unraveled at 10:17 a.m.

"By wisdom a house is built," Proverbs says, "and through understanding it is established." I didn't feel wise. I did feel called. I figured obedience counts for a lot in God's math.

Day 0 ½: The Space We Actually Have

I once thought a homeschool room required chalkboard walls, bunting, alphabet garlands, and a world map the size of Nebraska. You know what we had? One dining table with the varnish rubbed thin where elbows lived, a couch with a suspicious stain that is still a mystery, a porch that pretends it's a classroom every September and May, and the trunk of our van, which transforms into a mobile desk during soccer practice. Also: a toddler who believes all containers exist to be emptied.

So we set the table the way we set our days: simple and repeatable.

"Basket system," I announced, placing three woven baskets on the buffet like a magician revealing doves. "Morning Basket. Math. Creative."

"What's in Creative?" asked the thirteen-year-old, arching an eyebrow.

"Everything I'm brave enough to let you do without adult supervision for twenty minutes," I said. "Scissors live in this house by invitation only."

The baskets did not cure chaos. They corralled it. We added a Friday tidy ritual with music loud enough to drown the complaints. The baby learned to unload the Morning Basket with great joy; the four-year-old learned to reload it with great pride. The table stayed a table, for breakfast, phonics, paint, and spaghetti. The walls stayed ours, not a classroom's. But something shifted: the house began to feel like an invitation.

Time, Reimagined

The first week, I tried a six-period schedule, color-coded like a box of candy. By Tuesday it looked like a crime scene. The bell never rang because we don't own one and also because bell-ringing felt like pretending. The teens side-eyed me. The ten-year-old fidgeted a groove into his chair. I stood at the sink and, through tears I didn't want to admit to, prayed the shortest prayer I know: "Lord, help."

Then I remembered something I knew but had forgotten: we're not replicating school. We're reimagining education.

On a sheet of paper (spattered with something strawberry), I wrote a different plan:

- *Morning Time*, all together, Scripture + hymn + one living book + a poem

- *Core Blocks*, math/reading/writing, in ten- to twenty-minute sprints, rotated

- *Afternoons*, loop subjects (history, science, art, nature), projects, co-op

- *Evenings*, read-aloud or music, if we're awake enough to enjoy it

"Rhythm, not rigidity," I told them. "We'll protect the spine. Everything else bends."

I found a thrift-store bell that looks like it used to live at a church potluck table and set it by the fruit bowl. We rang it to change lanes, not to control time, but to bless it. The bell does not make our house efficient. It makes us smile. Sometimes that's holier.

When a math lesson imploded one morning (two kids crying, one of them me), I walked onto the porch, let the winter air slap me awake, and whispered, "Lord, help me see them how You do." It changed my tone. Not the lesson. But the air in the room lightened enough that we could breathe again.

A Plan, Not a Pile

Catalogs convinced me I needed twelve kinds of pencils, a magnetic timeline, scented markers, an abacus in three wood tones, and apparently a small shipping container. I bought...some of it. Then I sat in a drift of glossy workbooks and thought, *I've purchased a shelf of guilt.*

So I flipped the order. Goals first; tools second.

"What do we want to learn this fall?" I asked at dinner, pizza boxes a perfectly acceptable centerpiece.

"Multiplication," said the ten-year-old, mouth full. "But with basketball."

"Read harder books," said the fifteen-year-old. "On purpose."

"Draw real faces," said the thirteen-year-old, poking her sister's cheek. "Not just anime."

"Bake bread," said the seven-year-old solemnly, as if bread were a subject and also maybe a calling.

"Keep the baby alive," my husband added helpfully.

I wrote five simple goals on sticky notes and pressed them to the fridge door where expectations go to be sanctified.

Then we gathered tools like people who live in a real house and not a catalog. Library cards (plural). A battered thrift-store globe, the kind that still thinks the Soviet Union is holding a meeting. A used microscope missing a lens, which turned out to be fantastic because the kids learned more taking it apart than they ever would've peering through it. Pencils, paper, a glue stick battalion, a laptop that wheezes awake like a dinosaur, and curiosity. That was enough.

The best experiments still happen in the kitchen. We learned buoyancy by floating random objects in the bathtub. Educational and entertaining until someone dropped my phone in the water. It survived after a rice baptism and a lot of prayer. We counted it as science and testimony.

Teacher's Lounge

"You're going to need a teacher's lounge," my husband joked early on, and he was right. I just didn't know what it looked like yet.

A friend from church texted an address and a time: "Local co-op. Church basement. Come if you want. We all started scared." The baby and I arrived wearing three snacks and a hope.

The hallway smelled like coffee and crayons. Moms wedged toddlers on hips and talked about math like it wasn't a threat. A dad wheeled in a shop-vac and a box labeled "Engineering." Someone handed me a schedule and a smile. "You're new," she said gently. "Come stand by me. We have room."

I nearly cried in a room that doubles as a youth group hangout and a craft storage closet. Co-op is gloriously ordinary. We rotate teaching: Tasha does chemistry you can eat (marshmallow polymers changed my life), I handle writing (short lessons, big praise), another mom runs art with a joy that redeems every glitter spill. My kids learned to look a room in the eye and say, "Good morning," and then to stand up and present a bug report without whispering. I learned to ask for help *before* I crash.

The group text we started that day is now the soundtrack of my week:

Anyone have a copy of Story of the World, vol 2?Anyone want to join us at the museum at 10? Wednesday is free senior day, bring Grandma!Math meltdown here. Remind me this is normal.Normal. Deep breath. Bake cookies. Try again tomorrow.Praying now. Dropping soup at your door at 5.

Ecclesiastes says two are better than one. Turns out twenty can carry you when your printer dies and your courage wobbles.

NASA Lists and Refrigerator Theology

The summer before we started, I made a list that could launch rockets:

- Teach all subjects with excellence.

- Keep the house clean.

- Bake bread weekly.

- No screens before 3 p.m.

- Start piano lessons.

- Document everything beautifully.

- Also sleep.

By October I had checked one thing off: "Buy bread instead." I declared it a strategic pivot.

We swapped perfection for priorities. Each child set two or three quarterly goals. We wrote them on colored sticky notes and gave the refrigerator a job: hold us without shaming us. The ten-year-old's read, "Know all multiplication tables. Build model rocket. Be kind to sisters even when they're wrong." The fifteen-year-old's: "Finish *To Kill a Mockingbird.* Create a budget. Help with dinner Thursdays." The seven-year-old's: "Read *Little House* with Mom. Bake bread. Learn to whistle."

We made a "Victory List" on the inside of the pantry door next to Calling-Clarity-Courage. Whenever someone reached a goal, or even just overcame a day, we scribbled it down. "Finished first chapter book." "Presented bug report (with live beetle)." "No tears in math for three days in a row: confetti!" "Found the baby's shoe." The list grew long and crooked and holy.

Progress stopped sounding like grades. It started sounding like, "Mom, can I try one more time before you change it?" That sentence counts for more than any test I've ever seen.

Finding Our Heartbeat

At the beginning I tried on other people's philosophies like sweaters. Charlotte Mason fit our mornings like a cardigan: short lessons, living books, nature walks with pockets full of rocks and intentions. Classical gave the teens structure to hang their big thoughts on, grammar, logic, rhetoric, and the audacity to argue (kindly) with actual evidence. Unschooling on Fridays let curiosity lead: driveway "aquatic erosion" with a hose and two very muddy toddlers, a bread-baking challenge judged by Grandpa, a Shakespeare recital with pool noodles.

But I wanted our own heartbeat, something that could hum beneath any curriculum. So one Sunday evening we held a quick family meeting around popcorn and the hum of the dishwasher. "What do we want our school to *be*?" I asked.

"Kind," said the seven-year-old immediately, cheeks full.

"True," said a teen.

"Fun," said the ten-year-old. "And loud." (He's not wrong.)

We wrote a short mission on a sticky note because that's what we own in abundance: "In our home, learning is worship. We seek knowledge with curiosity, practice truth with grace, and remember wisdom begins with the fear of the Lord." We taped it inside the school cabinet next to the extra tape that never stays where it belongs. Deuteronomy 6 sits underneath it in my heart, teach them when you sit at home, when you walk along the road, when you lie down, when you get up. Turns out God wrote the best homeschool philosophy a long time ago.

Margin is a Spiritual Practice

One Tuesday, our schedule was perfect: math, reading, nature study, lunch, art. At 9:40, the baby spiked a fever. At 9:42, the Wi-Fi died like it had taken an oath. At 9:44, the dog threw up directly onto the history book in an act of literary criticism. I looked at the ceiling and practiced not crying.

I closed the book (carefully, using only the corners), made soup, and read *Little House in the Big Woods* out loud while the baby slept on my chest and the dog looked contrite. We called it school and meant it. The seven-year-old asked, "Is this allowed?" I thought of Proverbs 19:21 and said, "Yes. Many are the plans, kiddo. The Lord's purposes still prevail."

We started building margin on purpose: lighter Fridays for catch-up and errands; one "flex block" daily that could expand if a conversation grew wings; a standing rule that if everyone is fighting, we go outside. The moon rose early one afternoon, pale and brave in the blue, and we stood in the driveway with mugs and wonder, talking about phases and faithfulness. No worksheet would've held them the way the sky did.

"Mom," my oldest said one night, "you don't freak out anymore when stuff goes wrong." I laughed. "That's because I've had a lot of practice." Flexibility is not failure. It's trust made visible.

Learning Styles and Basketball Math

"Mom, my brain doesn't work that way," my son said during a spelling lesson that was mostly groaning. He wasn't being dramatic. He was being honest. The way I was teaching didn't match the way he learns.

That evening I read about visual, auditory, and kinesthetic learners with a pen in my hand, underlining, but also forgiving myself. The next morning we dragged spelling to the driveway and wrote words in chalk taller than the toddler. The ten-year-old added flames. The four-year-old added a dragon. Everyone remembered how to spell "through."

Math moved to the hoop. "Six times seven," I called. "Forty-two!" he yelled, ball arcing, swish. The thirteen-year-old narrated history back to me while sketching a famous eyebrow. The fifteen-year-old memorized Scripture while pacing. The seven-year-old learned to read holding the kitten like a diploma. We made room for the ways God knit them together, and the house relaxed like a held breath let go.

Paperwork in the Light

The legal pieces that once made me queasy became, strangely, an act of gratitude. We filed our intent, kept simple attendance, tuck photos and a line or two of description into a monthly portfolio. When the reminder arrived in the mail to submit next year's notice, I traced the path here, parents who fought boring, grinding battles so we could stack blocks with our babies at 10 a.m. on a Tuesday without glancing over our shoulders.

"Why do we have to send papers?" the seven-year-old asked.

"Because we live with neighbors," I said. "And because saying 'We're here and we're doing this with integrity' is a way to love them, too." She nodded like that made sense and went back to drawing a worm with a smile that was frankly optimistic.

Confidence, Bottled (If Only)

If I could bottle one thing for new homeschool moms, I'd hand out quiet confidence like elderberry syrup. Not the loud *I've-got-this* kind, but the steady *God's-got-us* kind. Mine grew in centimeters: one good morning time after three clumsy ones, one "I'm sorry" offered to a child I snapped at, one portfolio page completed while everyone miraculously entertained themselves for nine minutes.

We started a Victory Jar, index cards folded and dropped in whenever someone accomplished something that felt like climbing a personal mountain. At the end of each quarter, we poured them out like confetti. "Finished first novel." "Stayed kind during sibling meltdown." "Built rocket that actually launched (and did not hit the neighbor's roof)." "Mom didn't cry about math once this week." We laughed. I blinked back tears, the happy kind. Philippians 1:6 came to sit next to me: *He who began a good work in you will carry it on to completion.* I believed it for them first. I am slowly believing it for me.

One evening the thirteen-year-old slid onto the counter while I chopped onions. "I like learning from you," she said, picking at a sticker the dishwasher will never surrender. "You always believe I can figure it out."

I put the knife down. "That's because you can," I said, voice wobbling on the edges. And then I realized the thing I hadn't known at the beginning: the confidence God was growing in me was seeding itself in them.

The Day the Plan Worked (and Why That's Not the Point)

For the record, there are days that hum. The bell rings, the reading is rich, someone quotes a psalm without being asked, the math clicks, the toddler naps, the dog behaves like a citizen, and the lunch is both edible and on time. We had one of those the week after the dog-vomit incident, and I stood at the sink at 11:47 a.m., hands in hot water and gratitude, and thought, *Oh. This, too, is school.*

But the point of preparation isn't to force days into submission. It's to build a floor strong enough to catch you when you fall and spring you when you leap. Calling, clarity, courage. Baskets. Rhythms. A plan that bends. A people who answer texts. Sticky notes that tell the truth. A mission taped inside a cabinet with the extra tape. A pantry door that holds your victories and your whys. A God who meets you in the kitchen with a candle that insists light belongs here.

That night, after the kids drifted to their rooms and the house held its soft noises, the hum, the click, the sigh, I stood at the pantry and traced the three words with my finger like a prayer: Calling. Clarity. Courage. Then I wrote one more on a new card and slid it beside them.

Faithfulness.

Not perfect, but faithful. That's the foundation under our feet.

Tomorrow I will set out pencils like small promises. Someone will pocket one within nine seconds. The baby will clap. The ten-year-old will ask if basketball counts as math (yes, again). The teenagers will argue about a thesis and whether it can wink (I think so). Someone will cry. Someone will apologize. We will ring the bell and move lanes, we will eat fractions in cookie form, we will walk around the block and name three trees, we will send one text to the co-op thread that simply says, "Pray," and three will arrive back, "On it." We will tape another sticky note to the fridge: "Read together on the porch." We will keep the jars and the binders and the baskets, but mostly we will keep the peace we're learning to guard.

Preparation didn't make us perfect. It made us ready to love each other on purpose when the plan didn't love us back.

And at 11:47, when I look around the table and see crumbs and courage in equal measure, I will touch the bell, smile at the people God gave me, and say the sentence that steadies our house:

"That's enough for today."

daily homeschooling life & crafting your family's rhythm

the beauty of an ordinary day

If you asked ten homeschool moms to describe a "typical day," most would pause, grin, and say, "Well, it depends." Then they'd tell you a story. Because homeschooling isn't a looped schedule; it's a living thing. It grows with the seasons, the babies, the bumpy nights, the new interests, and the unexpected opportunities. It has a heartbeat.

Here's how it sounds in our house on a Tuesday in January: the coffee grinder whirs before the sun rises. I pull on a sweater and step over yesterday's tower of blocks, left on the rug like a small city. Upstairs, someone is singing off-key in the shower. Our ten-year-old is already dressed because he has decided this is the year he becomes "a morning person." The seventeen-year-old pads in, bleary but cheerful, and asks if we have any more of the cinnamon bread. The baby calls from her crib. The dog barks at nothing in particular, which is his morning devotion.

Within ten minutes the kitchen smells like toast, and there's a line for butter. Someone remembers they never found their math notebook yesterday. Someone else needs a paper towel. I pour my coffee and whisper a quick prayer I say almost every morning: "Lord, lead us gently today."

By the time everyone arrives at the table, the room is imperfectly ready, crumbs still on the floor, crayons in a jar, a candle waiting. I've learned that being "ready" in homeschooling doesn't mean spotless. It means willing. It means showing up with the best of who you are and trusting God to meet you in the rest.

Early on, I tried to run our home like the bell schedule I remember from high school. I printed a color-coded plan: math at 8:00, reading at 8:45, writing at 9:30. It survived until 8:22, when orange juice baptized the page. That was the day I learned an important truth: our home runs on connection, not the clock.

We began practicing "anchoring." Anchors are not timestamps; they're touchpoints. Breakfast. Morning time. Lunch. Quiet reading. Dinner. These repeat, no matter the season. Lessons flow between them. On strong days we move along with ease. On choppy days we cling to those anchors to steady ourselves.

Most of our magic hides in the ordinary. It looks like a seven-year-old curled into the corner of the couch with a stack of picture books. It sounds like a teen reading a paragraph aloud to a younger sibling and explaining a tricky sentence without being asked. It feels like the kitchen table after a good conversation: pencil shavings, smudged eraser crumbs, a page with ideas scratched in the margins. If I pause and look, I can see it, learning, yes, but also a family turning toward one another on purpose.

There are mornings when nothing goes smoothly. We burn the toast. Someone cries over long division. I realize I forgot to thaw the chicken. Still, a strange peace settles when we lean back into rhythm. I tell myself the same phrase I've told countless new moms: "Faithfulness over frenzy." The work that matters most rarely looks impressive. It looks like showing up again, with gentleness, for the next thing.

morning time: the heart of connection

Morning time became the center of our homeschool by accident. I wanted a way to gather everyone before the day ran away from us. We started small: a candle, a short Scripture reading, a poem, and prayer. The baby sat in her high chair and banged a spoon. The four-year-old held a crayon like a trophy. Somehow, it still felt holy.

We rotate what we read. Some days it's a Psalm and a chapter from a family read-aloud. On other days we add a piece of history or a short biography. In December, hymns fill the kitchen. In April, poetry slips in while tulips lean toward the light. My only rule is this: keep it short enough to succeed, rich enough to remember.

On a recent Monday, the ten-year-old asked, "Can I pick the poem today?" He chose one about winter fields and heavy clouds. The words slowed us. We sat quieter than usual. The teen took a picture of the sky an hour later because it looked like the poem. That's what morning time does, plants seeds. Not all bloom the same day, but they root us.

Connection matters more than compliance. Some mornings the toddler draws happy faces on sticky notes and delivers them down the line like party favors. Sometimes the seven-year-old counts the candles in the Advent wreath three times before we move on. Occasionally the baby cries right in the middle of Psalm 23 and nobody remembers where we left off. I used to feel interrupted; now I feel reminded. We're forming people, not checking boxes.

After the candle is blown out, we scatter. The seventeen-year-old opens her laptop for algebra and literature. The fifteen-year-old reviews chemistry while I sit beside the thirteen-year-old for writing. The ten-year-old finishes a chapter in history, then practices piano. The seven-year-old reads aloud from a beginning reader while the four-year-old builds something ambitious with magnets. The baby roams like a happy inspector and occasionally confiscates a pencil.

When we miss morning time, I notice the edges of the day fray a little faster. When we keep it, the tone of the house softens. It doesn't guarantee smooth lessons, but it reminds us why we're here. Education isn't only information. It's formation. It's hearts turned toward what is true and lovely, together.

If you're new to morning time, start with one piece you love. Read a Psalm. Sing a verse of a hymn. Light a candle and thank God for the day. Keep it simple, especially at first. I've learned that beauty doesn't compete with noise; it visits wherever it's welcomed.

balancing academics and real life

When we began homeschooling, I believed school had to live between 8 and 3, Monday through Friday. I believed learning wore neat labels and sat politely in subject-sized bins. Then life introduced me to a different teacher: experience.

On a gray afternoon we baked banana bread. The seven-year-old read the recipe and measured flour. The ten-year-old doubled the ingredients and worked out fractions on the back of an envelope. The teen explained why baking soda and vinegar fizz. We waited by the oven and talked about the chemistry of heat. The house smelled like cinnamon and a conversation none of us planned.

A clear night invited jackets and a thermos. We stepped into the backyard and found Orion. The ten-year-old recognized Betelgeuse from a book he'd devoured. The thirteen-year-old asked how far light travels in a year. We talked about distances so large that numbers folded in on themselves. Nobody was yawning. Learning stretched its legs under the stars.

A report I read noted that many homeschoolers spend more time in hands-on experiences than their peers in traditional classrooms. I didn't need the statistic to tell me what I already saw: our richest lessons often take place away from worksheets. The museum docent who lets a child handle a fossil. The neighbor who tells stories from a war we only knew in dates. The garden bed where seeds teach patience without saying a word.

Real life refuses to wait for open spaces on the calendar. The dishwasher floods; the toddler spikes a fever; a friend needs a last-minute meal. For a while, those moments felt like interruptions. Now they feel like part of the plan. Dishes teach responsibility. Sibling disagreements teach repentance and repair. A long drive to the doctor becomes a rolling seminar in geography, prayer, and gratitude for Tylenol.

So my metric changed. When a day unravels, I ask two questions: Did we learn something that matters? Did we stay connected? If the answers lean toward yes, I can sleep.

Academics still matter. We study grammar and math on purpose. We write essays. We memorize facts. But we hold all of it inside a larger story: we are a family learning how to live wisely and love well. The checklist only gets to be the map; it never gets to be the destination.

the gift of flexibility (and the myth of control)

One Tuesday last spring, I decided we were going to have a perfect school day. I set out sharpened pencils, pulled books, wrote cheerful notes in the margins of my plan. By ten o'clock the toddler had painted the dog, the Wi-Fi crashed, two children argued over a ruler, and my cheerful notes felt like satire.

I stood at the sink, hands in soapy water, and laughed the kind of laugh that teeters between humor and tears. Then I turned off the water and called everyone back to the table. "New plan," I said. "We're moving to the porch. The sun is out. Bring your books and a blanket."

On the porch, peace returned. The seven-year-old sounded out words beside a pot of herbs. The ten-year-old sketched a maple tree. The teen wrote a page she'd been avoiding. The breeze moved. My shoulders dropped.

Homeschooling keeps telling me the same truth in different ways: control is smaller than I imagine, and trust is sturdier than I expect. The more tightly I grip the plan, the more brittle the day becomes. When I hold the plan with open hands, adjustments feel like invitations, not failures.

Flexibility is not the absence of structure; it is the presence of wisdom. We keep our anchors. We aim for steady. We also leave room for weather, wonder, and real needs. A thunderstorm turns into a lesson on fronts and pressure. A rabbit trail in history leads to pioneer journals and a pan of cornbread. A sad morning requires tea and a slower pace. These are not detours from learning. They are learning.

Proverbs says many plans live in a person's heart, but the Lord's purpose stands. I write plans anyway because structure serves us. Yet I've learned to watch for God's quiet redirections. The day I let go of "perfect," our home felt lighter. The work did not shrink; it breathed.

If you woke today to chaos, you are not doing it wrong. You are living a real life in a real house with real people. Adjust what you can. Let go of what you cannot. Save a piece of the plan for tomorrow. Grace fits more than you think.

crafting a rhythm that nurtures peace

Every home hums with a rhythm, whether intentional or accidental. In our early months I lived in accidental rhythm: late starts, scattered meals, papers in a drifting stack that followed me from room to room. At night I climbed in bed and felt like I'd been running all day without knowing where the finish line was.

An older mom watched me scramble and said gently, "You don't need more hours. You need a song your day can sing." I didn't understand at first. She explained that rhythm isn't a strict schedule. It is a pattern you can remember even when life grows loud.

We began with mornings. Before lessons, we tidy the kitchen for five minutes. Not to impress anyone, only to give our brains a clear table to land on. We light the candle. We read. We pray. The baby throws a spoon. The four-year-old lines up crayons like parade floats. It is enough.

Midday invites focus. I keep the heaviest work before lunch: math, reading, writing. Everyone knows this, so their energy bends toward it. One day it takes an hour; another day it takes two and a half. I try to watch faces as much as I watch the clock. If someone's shoulders ride near their ears, I suggest a stretch. If we need a reset, we walk to the mailbox.

Afternoons loosen. We save them for projects, nature, co-op, music, and chores. The ten-year-old builds a small catapult and measures the arc of pennies. The seven-year-old paints with water on the driveway and announces she is an artist because "my canvas dries itself." The teens meet online with a writing group run by a friend from church. Sometimes we visit the library and come home with more books than arms.

Evenings belong to family. We eat together most nights, even if the table includes a half-finished puzzle. After dishes, we choose one shared thing: a chapter from a read-aloud, a board game, a walk in the cool. When the house settles, I jot a few notes about the day, three lines at most. I do it to remember, but also to see the faithfulness threaded through small things.

We also plan rest on purpose. Once every few weeks we keep a "margin day." No formal lessons. We make muffins, catch up on laundry, visit a grandparent, or simply clean the corners that collect life. Guilt used to knock on those days. Now it doesn't stay long. Rest makes the rest of it work.

Psalm 90 says to number our days so we gain wisdom. For me, numbering our days looks like leaving white space. It looks like choosing less so the right things have room to grow. The more I protect our simple anchors, the more peace visits our home.

handling interruptions with grace

For a long time, I believed interruptions were the enemy of education. Then I noticed how often God taught us during the moments I did not plan.

We were deep into a history lesson about colonial winters when the seven-year-old pressed her face to the window and said, "The mail truck is sliding." We pulled on boots and ran outside. The tires spun in the slush. The teen and I pushed while the ten-year-old threw sand from the yard under the wheels. The truck eased forward. The driver rolled down the window and laughed with relief. "You saved me," he said. The seven-year-old waved like a parade queen.

Back inside, we dried gloves on the register and talked about friction and momentum. We wrote a thank-you note for his work in bad weather. That afternoon stuck longer than the names and dates on the page. The lesson was service and science and neighborliness at once.

Another day the dog ate a spelling list. I considered despair and chose humor. We retold the words from memory and turned it into a game. The four-year-old offered to test us because "I'm very good at asking questions." We laughed. The list survived in spirit, and so did the mood.

Interruptions reveal the curriculum we didn't know we needed. When the baby cries during Bible reading, we learn compassion in motion. When a neighbor stops by, hospitality steps off the page. When a teenager wakes fragile and quiet, we learn to set aside the plan and make room for a long walk.

A small practice helped me: when the day tilts, I pause and ask, "What is the real lesson right now?" Sometimes the answer is patience. Sometimes it is perseverance through a dull chapter. Sometimes it is mercy. These are not secondary outcomes. They are core work. No textbook does them better than a living moment.

making space for rest and joy

Burnout rarely announces itself. It arrives quietly, layered, in small withdrawals you don't notice at first. One week you're humming through lessons. The next, you're staring at a stack of unsharpened pencils, convinced you are failing everyone you love.

Rest is not a treat for after everything is finished. Rest is fuel for the middle. God rested on the seventh day long before anyone needed a teacher in a kitchen. He built rhythm into creation for humans who confuse their worth with their output.

In our home, Sundays are simple. Church, slow lunch, naps, and something easy for dinner, often pancakes. No grading. No planning. Sometimes a walk if the weather forgives. The house exhales.

We tuck little rests into the week, too. On Wednesday afternoons we sometimes trade math drills for a board game. Fractions still appear when someone divides the last slice of banana bread. On a mild evening we choose ice cream after dinner and practice gratitude on the drive. These moments are not a retreat from learning. They are the kind of air learning needs to keep breathing.

Joy returns easiest when I remember our why. On weary days I pull our read-aloud from the shelf and build a blanket fort. We read by flashlight and drink cocoa. The seven-year-old asks, "Can we do school like this every day?" I smile because we are doing school; it just happens to include a couch cushion roof.

Joy also grows in tiny rituals. Lighting a candle during morning time. Playing the same instrumental song while we clean up after lunch. Putting a flower in a jar on the table even when dinner is pasta and jarred sauce. These small gestures tell our minds what our hearts forget: this work is good and worth savoring.

If joy feels far, don't go hunting for a grand fix. Choose one small thing that makes you breathe deeper, a walk to the mailbox, a phone call to a friend, a prayer whispered in the pantry. Joy often slips in through small doors.

embracing imperfection and celebrating grace

There will be tears in this life, yours and theirs. There will be days you scroll through someone else's photos and wonder how their house gleams and their children appear thrilled about Latin declensions. I promise you they have laundry piles too.

One Friday after a week of false starts, I sat on the back steps with my Bible open to 2 Corinthians 12. "My grace is sufficient for you, for My power is made perfect in weakness." I read it out loud because sometimes the heart listens better through the ears. Then I prayed a short prayer: "Lord, help me stop striving. Help me receive."

Receiving grace changed the way I measured our days. I stopped asking, "Was it perfect?" I began asking, "Were we faithful?" Faithfulness sounds ordinary: I apologized when I snapped. I hugged the child who stretched every ounce of me that morning. I admitted I didn't know the answer and suggested we look it up together. I wrote a note to a teenager whose quiet diligence deserved celebration. I made eggs for dinner and called it good.

Grace looks like trying again tomorrow without dragging today's shame behind you. It looks like trusting that learning can happen in a room with Lego land mines and a sink full of spoons. It looks like telling your children, "I'm still growing too," and seeing their shoulders relax because they are allowed to be in progress as well.

When we model grace, our children learn resilience. They see that failure isn't the final word; it's the soil where growth takes root. They learn that repentance isn't a punishment; it's a way back to each other. The atmosphere of a home changes when grace is the rule and not the exception.

Some evenings, after everyone is asleep, I walk through the quiet rooms and gather the day's remnants: a pencil on the stairs, a sock under a chair, a book left open to a sentence someone loved. I feel tired, but also full. Not of perfection, of presence. Of the sense that God met us in the middle again.

where real learning lives

Homeschooling is not a quest for flawless days. It is a daily turning toward what matters in the middle of a real life. You will teach phonics and fractions. You will also teach patience in long checkout lines, curiosity in the backyard, forgiveness at the kitchen sink, and joy on a Wednesday when the sun returns.

Take this chapter as your permission to exhale. Build a rhythm that fits your family. Let interruptions become lessons. Protect rest. Watch for joy. Tell the story of your days to yourself so you can see the grace threaded through them.

When the house finally quiets and the books are stacked, step into the doorway of the room where you taught and prayed and tried. Take a deep breath. Whisper thanks. You did the work you were called to do.

Not perfectly. Faithfully. And that is enough.

my story: a random tuesday

On a Tuesday in January, the coffee grinder whirred before the sun remembered Minnesota. I pulled on a sweater big enough to count as a hug and stepped over yesterday's block city left in the living room like a skyline. Upstairs, water ran; somebody sang one brave note and abandoned the melody. The dog performed his daily ritual, two barks at nothing and a full-body shake that sounded like maracas. The baby, one and a half and convinced she is the mayor, called from her crib, "Mamaaaaa," as if I'd been ignoring her for days.

By the time I reached the kitchen, the ten-year-old, our sole boy and our unofficial head of R&D, was dressed and inspecting the frost on the window with a magnifying glass. "Morning person era," he announced, as if rebranding. The seventeen-year-old padded in, bleary and cheerful, and asked about the last slice of cinnamon bread. The fifteen-year-old wandered after, hair in a bun that declared independence. The thirteen-year-old, who claims she can't think before tea, found a mug and gave me a look that said today was going to require extra gentleness. The seven-year-old arrived with two socks that did not match and a face that did. The four-year-old asked the daily question, "Can I stir?" and reached for the wooden spoon before I answered.

The kitchen organized itself the way kitchens do when they've learned a family's rhythm: kettle, toaster, clatter of bowls, a line for butter. Someone couldn't find a math notebook. Someone else needed a paper towel urgently for reasons that turned out to be very small and very sticky. I poured coffee and whispered the prayer I usually do: "Lord, lead us gently today."

Our table was imperfectly ready, crumbs on the floor, crayons in a jar, today's books stacked with ambition. I used to think ready meant spotless. Now it means willing. I touched the little brass bell that sits by the fruit bowl and watched their faces turn to me, a chorus I can't conduct but get to love.

"Good morning," I said. "Let's anchor."

Early on, I tried to run our home like the bell schedule in my memory. I even printed a color-coded plan once: math at 8:00, reading at 8:45, writing at 9:30. It survived until 8:22, when orange juice baptized the page and the four-year-old sobbed because the color orange was "too loud." That was the day I learned an ordinary truth that changed our atmosphere: our home runs on connection, not the clock.

So we started practicing anchors instead of timestamps: breakfast, morning time, lunch, quiet reading, dinner. These repeat like the chorus of a favorite song. Lessons flow between them. On strong days, we glide. On choppy days, we grip the rope and let it steady us.

"Candle?" the seven-year-old asked. I nodded. She lit it with the seriousness of a surgeon and set it between the oatmeal and the stack of readers. I opened to Psalm 90 and read a few verses, slow enough that the littles could breathe with the words. We prayed a short prayer everyone knows by heart: "Jesus, direct our steps." The baby banged a spoon like a cymbal. Somehow, it still felt holy.

"Poem?" the ten-year-old said. He had one ready, a winter piece with heavy clouds and stubble fields. The words slowed us. The seventeen-year-old took a picture of the sky an hour later because it looked like the poem. That's what morning time does: plants seeds. Not all bloom the same day, but the roots make a net under the whole week.

I call morning time "the heart" because it reminds us what we're doing here. Education isn't only information; it's formation. We aren't just filling minds; we're training hearts to turn to what is true and lovely, together, even with a baby campaign banging in the background.

After the candle, we scattered. The seventeen-year-old opened her laptop for algebra and literature, she works best at a clip I can't keep up with anymore, which is part of the joy. The fifteen-year-old curled at the end of the table with chemistry. I slid next to the thirteen-year-old for writing. The ten-year-old finished a chapter in history, then moved to the piano with a seriousness that makes me smile. The seven-year-old read to me from a beginning reader, tracing under each word with a finger that still has marker in the fingernail. The four-year-old built a magnet tower on the floor, narrating the drama of its collapse. The baby roamed like an inspector and occasionally confiscated a pencil as if for the public good.

That is the beauty of our ordinary day: a table that contains algebra and phonics and toast crumbs at the same time. If I stop and look, I can see it, learning, yes, but also something harder to measure: a family turning toward one another on purpose.

By ten, the spell frayed. The ten-year-old got snagged on long division and slid dramatically under his chair. The thirteen-year-old's essay hit the part where every sentence looks like a mistake. The four-year-old insisted the only acceptable snack was the one currently frozen solid. The dog chose violence and stole a mitten. The baby whined. I felt my shoulders creeping toward my ears.

"Pause," I said, to them and to myself. We stood up and did ten jumping jacks, including the baby, who bounced like a happy lemon. We walked to the mailbox. The air bit our noses. The seven-year-old caught snowflakes on her tongue and declared herself a scientist. By the time we came back, the edges of our day had softened enough to continue.

"New plan," I announced. "Bring your books to the porch. The sun is pretending to be brave. Let's meet it."

This is the part I didn't understand at the start: flexibility isn't the absence of structure; it's the presence of wisdom. We keep our anchors. We aim for steady. We also leave room for weather, wonder, and real needs. A perfect plan makes me brittle. An open hand makes me kind.

On the porch, peace returned. The seven-year-old sounded out words beside a pot of herbs. The ten-year-old sketched the maple tree's bones. The teen wrote a page she'd been avoiding. The breeze moved; my shoulders dropped. "It's like the air is smarter out here," the thirteen-year-old said. I nodded. "Mine too."

At eleven, I rang the bell and called everyone back to the table for math sprints. We do them in ten-minute bursts so nobody gets lost in the forest of a page. The ten-year-old answered times facts out loud while pivoting from the stove to the sink. "Six times seven?" I called, a basketball coach at the line. "Forty-two!" he yelled, satisfying swish. The seven-year-old counted by fives with a jump rope. The four-year-old lined up raisins in sets of two and ate her work, which is the kind of assessment I feel good about. The fifteen-year-old timed herself for a set on radicals then celebrated like she'd beaten a personal best. "Math is just a puzzle with manners," she said.

At lunchtime we practiced a different kind of arithmetic. We doubled a banana bread recipe, and fractions became friendly. The seven-year-old measured flour; the ten-year-old worked out halves and quarters on the back of an envelope. The fifteen-year-old explained why baking soda and vinegar fizz like a middle-school dance. We peeked through the oven door and talked about heat and patience. The house smelled like cinnamon and a conversation none of us planned. Real life refuses to stay in subject-sized bins, and I'm learning that's not a bug; it's a feature.

After lunch, the baby went down for a nap that would either last twelve minutes or a thousand years. (It was nineteen. We lived.) The four-year-old spread a blanket on the floor and declared it an art studio. The ten-year-old asked for the good tape and the "unsupervised scissors," which is not a phrase that exists. I said yes to tape and found the safer scissors. The teens moved to their afternoon loop, history on Tuesdays, science on Wednesdays, art on Thursdays. The thirteen-year-old has been devouring pioneer journals, so she pulled me into a rabbit trail about how to leaven bread without packets. We set aside time next week to try sourdough like it was 1850. "You'll hate it," the fifteen-year-old said cheerfully. "You like rules." "True," I admitted. "But I like you more."

Midafternoon comes with options: library, nature walk, co-op, music, chores. Today it brought a library run. We left the house in that slow, clumsy migration every large family knows. Boots, hats, mittens, a baby in a puffy suit that turns her into a starfish. The seven-year-old grabbed our tote bag and gave me a look of profound seriousness. "We need more biographies," she said. "I like when people are real."

At the library, the ten-year-old found a book about Orion and became a docent on the spot. "Betelgeuse," he whispered reverently, like telling a secret. The thirteen-year-old located a collection of poems she'd heard at co-op and hugged it like a friend. The four-year-old selected a book about a bear and pizza and announced she was learning Italian because pizza is Italian. The baby toddled past a display and "reshelved" three books onto the floor; we apologized and picked them up with penitent speed. The librarian smiled. "It's good to see you," she said, like a benediction. I smiled back because that is one of our favorite sentences.

Back home, the afternoon opened the door to interruptions that used to feel like enemies and now feel like a class the Lord scheduled Himself. At 3:10, the mail truck spun its wheels in the slush outside. The seven-year-old pressed her face to the window: "He's stuck." Boots on. Sand from the yard under the tires. The teen and I pushed; the ten-year-old directed like a foreman. The truck caught, rolled forward. The driver laughed and waved. "You saved me," he said. Back inside, we dried our gloves on the register and talked about friction and momentum and neighborliness. We wrote him a thank-you note for working in bad weather. The lesson stuck longer than any date on a page.

At 3:40, the dog ate a spelling list. I considered despair and chose humor. We reconstructed it from memory and turned it into a game show. The four-year-old volunteered as host because "I am very good at asking questions." "Use it in a sentence," she demanded of the ten-year-old, who looked at the ceiling and improvised something about astronauts and muffins. We laughed. The list survived in spirit; so did the mood.

When the toddlers of our house (there is always one) interrupt Bible reading with shrieks, I used to feel robbed of the holiness. Now I realize: compassion in motion might be the holiest thing we do all day. When a neighbor stops by with a need, hospitality steps off the page and into the doorway. When a teenager wakes fragile and quiet, curriculum makes space for a walk, because the person is always the point.

Rhythm has taught me to ask a small, saving question when a day tilts: *What is the real lesson right now?* Sometimes it's perseverance through a dull chapter. Sometimes it's patience, which I dislike practicing. Sometimes it's mercy. These are not side quests. They are core work. No textbook does them better than a living moment.

Evenings belong to family, as much as we can make it so. We ate dinner with a half-finished puzzle on the end of the table because that is a perfect metaphor for us. We told the day in small pieces, best part, hard part, funny moment. The ten-year-old said his best part was pushing the mail truck. The thirteen-year-old's hard part was cutting a paragraph she loved. The fifteen-year-old's funny moment was the dog's face after swallowing the spelling list; she did the impression so well the seven-year-old snorted water.

After dishes, we chose a shared thing, tonight, a chapter from our read-aloud by lamplight. The four-year-old built a blanket fort that successfully trapped the cat. The baby toddled circles around the ottoman and fell into my lap with an oomph. The teens read alternate pages, and I watched their faces turn serious at the same sentence. Story does that, the communal hush, the room leaning in, the way the world narrows and widens at once.

We clean up to the same instrumental song every night, a small ritual that tells the house it's time to exhale. I tucked the littles with the ordinary liturgy: water, one more hug, whisper of a verse, "You are loved. You are safe." The seven-year-old asked if we could do school in a fort tomorrow. I said, "Maybe," because hope is a good bedtime snack.

When the house fell to its nighttime hum, heater, fridge, the quiet creak of old wood, I walked through and gathered the day's remnants: a pencil on the stairs, a sock under a chair, a book left open to a sentence someone loved. I jotted three lines in my tiny log:

- Pushed mail truck = friction + service

- Poem morning / sky afternoon = connection

- Dog ate spelling (again) = laughter saved us

Those notes are a mercy to future me on days when it feels like nothing happened. Numbering our days isn't about tallying victories; it's about noticing grace.

Before bed, I stood in the pantry doorway where our cards live, the ones that say *Calling. Clarity. Courage.* and our little mission: *In our home, learning is worship. We seek knowledge with curiosity, practice truth with grace, and remember wisdom begins with the fear of the Lord.* I touched the edges like a prayer. I'm not building a perfect schedule. I'm building a song our days can sing even when my voice is tired.

Sundays are our long rest, church, lunch, naps, pancakes for dinner, no grading. But we tuck little rests into the week, too: a Wednesday board game that becomes a stealth fractions lesson, a walk at dusk, ice cream after a hard appointment. Rest isn't a prize we earn; it's fuel we need. God built rhythm into creation for people like me who confuse worth with output. When joy feels far, I don't go hunting for a grand fix. I choose one small door: a candle, a text to a friend, a Psalm whispered in the pantry. Joy slips in like it was always waiting.

I don't want to pretend our days are smooth. There are tears, mine and theirs. There are weeks when everything feels like a false start and the laundry becomes a mountain range. There are moments I scroll a stranger's luminous photos and forget that no one posts the smell of the trash can. On a Friday like that, I sat on the back steps with my Bible open to 2 Corinthians 12 and read it aloud because sometimes my heart believes my ears more than my eyes: "My grace is sufficient for you, for My power is made perfect in weakness." I prayed a small prayer: "Lord, help me stop striving. Help me receive."

Receiving grace changed how I measured success. I stopped asking, "Was it perfect?" I started asking, "Were we faithful?" Faithfulness sounds ordinary. I apologized when I snapped. I hugged the child who stretched every last ounce of me at 10:06 a.m. I admitted I didn't know and looked it up with them, which is not a failure but an education. I wrote a note to a teenager whose quiet diligence deserved notice. I made eggs for dinner and called it sufficient. Grace let us try again without dragging shame from yesterday like a backpack full of rocks.

We keep a "Victory Jar" on the shelf. It's a thrift-store mason jar full of folded index cards, a record of tiny wins: "Finished first chapter book." "Stood up to present bug report with live beetle guest." "No tears in math all week." "Helped neighbor in snow." "Mom didn't cry over printer jam." On margin days, those planned breathers we tuck into the calendar so life has room, we pour the cards out and read them like a feast. It's not about bragging. It's about remembering. The jar says what my heart forgets: progress rarely arrives in grand gestures. It walks in on little feet.

If you asked me for our typical day, I would grin and say, "Well, it depends," and then I'd tell you this story. Because our days are a living thing. They grow with seasons, babies, bumpy nights, new interests, unexpected opportunities. They have a heartbeat.

Most nights, when everyone is finally horizontal and the dog has given up on glory, I stand in the doorway of the room where we did the work, taught and prayed and tried, and let the quiet tell me the truth I keep relearning: real learning lives in the middle of real life. It lives in banana bread math and Orion's shoulders, in a mail truck stuck in slush and a poem that made a teenager look up, in morning candles and evening dishes, in a mother who is still being taught.

I touch the bell one more time, a small benediction on the day, and turn off the light.

Not perfectly. Faithfully. And that is enough.

teaching multiple ages and stages, grace in the chaos

the table that never stayed clean

There's a glossy picture people carry in their minds when they hear the word *home-school*: tidy desks, color-coded folders, happy children bent over perfect copy work while a peaceful mother reads poetry in a sunbeam. It's charming. It's also not our house.

Our school lives at the kitchen table, the same table where pancakes stick to the griddle on Saturdays, where we fold laundry into lopsided piles, where someone is always building a cardboard city or taping feathers to a paper crown. There is a faint constellation of glitter in the wood grain that no amount of scrubbing can remove. I stopped trying years ago and decided to call it "permanent starlight."

By 8:30, the table fills with every stage of childhood. The high schooler settles in first, earbuds out, laptop open, a stack of notecards for her *To Kill a Mockingbird* essay. The middle schooler brings a spiral notebook, loses the pencil, finds the pencil behind his ear, and announces that today he likes fractions again. Two elementary kids slide chairs too loudly, unfurl a map of ancient Egypt, and argue cheerfully about whether the Nile looks like a snake or a zipper. The preschooler practices cutting "snowflakes," which is sometimes code for trimming her own bangs. The toddler arrives like a parade marshal, waving a wooden spoon.

The room hums like a radio tuned to seven stations at once. Somewhere in that hum, learning begins.

At first glance, the scene looks messy. On my better days, I breathe and look again. A teen quotes Atticus Finch while a little sister whispers the alphabet to a stuffed bear. A brother explains how to find a common denominator and uses Lego bricks to make his case. The baby smears banana on the high chair tray and claps for herself as if she has solved world hunger. These are not the kinds of moments that fit neatly on a test. These are the ones that form character: waiting your turn, helping a sibling, being kind when you're tired.

For a long time I believed good homeschooling required a clean table. Then one day, while I tried for the fourth time to explain why four-sixths simplifies to two-thirds, I noticed my oldest slide her chair toward her brother. She didn't sigh. She didn't correct him sharply. She asked, "Want to see a shortcut?" He nodded. She used slices of an apple to show the same whole represented in smaller parts. He grinned as it clicked. I stood there, dish towel in my hands, and felt my eyes sting. That quiet exchange said what the neatest room could not.

The table is sacred not because it's spotless, but because it holds us all. We eat here, pray here, argue here, forgive here. Sometimes we tape the paper over a sticky patch and keep going. Sometimes we push the books aside and bring out ice water and slices of oranges because the air inside feels heavy. The work of teaching many ages often looks like this, imperfect, honest, alive.

When I remember to breathe and look for it, that's the voice I hear in the middle of the mess: *This is working.*

learning to juggle without dropping the child

When there are many grades under one roof, the day can feel like a triage line: Who needs me most right now? Who can fly solo for fifteen minutes? Who is melting quietly behind a book? I used to try to teach every child everything at the same time. I nearly lost my mind and the joy that brought us to this life in the first place.

What helped was learning to gather where we can and release where we must. We start the morning all together. Bibles open. A short psalm. A simple prayer. Sometimes a hymn we half-remember and half-hum. The toddler adds percussion with a spoon on the table. The preschooler distributes crayons like party favors. It still counts.

After that, we do "family learning." History lends itself to this, so does science. One month we live in pyramids and papyrus, tasting dates in the afternoon and building a model shaduf by the back steps. The older kids research and write, the younger ones draw and narrate, the littlest stick stickers of camels in improbable places and listen with big eyes. Another month we move westward across a scratch-off map, reading pioneer journals, measuring out flour for cornbread, and watching the way a fire eats through a log. Everyone touches the story at their own level.

Grouping isn't complicated; it's merciful. For the subjects that must be individual, math, writing, upper-level science, we split. I keep a simple rotation and let each child know when it's their "front-row time." They look forward to it, because it means I'm fully theirs for a little while.

A few practical habits steadied the juggle:

Shared subjects first. When the energy is fresh, we do the together work. It gathers us before scattering us.

A quiet cue. We set a small lamp on the counter. Lamp on means "Mom is with a student." Everyone else uses quiet baskets or independent work. Lamp off means questions are welcome.

Mentor moments. Big kids become helpers in natural ways. "Can you listen to your sister's narration?" "Show him how you outline a paragraph." They're not miniature teachers; they're siblings practicing generosity and leadership.

One morning I caught myself spiraling, baby crying, someone stuck on long division, someone else asking for a thesis statement, the dog scratching at the door. I heard the familiar tightening in my chest. A thought came clear and kind: *You're not supposed to hold it all. Hold the one in front of you.* So I did. I changed the diaper. I took a breath. I returned to the math page and touched the boy's shoulder and said, "We'll take it one step at a time." The others waited. Not perfectly, but patiently enough. Faithfulness looks like that most days, the next problem, the next sandwich, the next small mercy.

there is no balance & that's ok

I chased balance as if it were a trophy I could earn. If I organized more, scheduled better, tried harder, surely I could meet every need evenly. Balance, in my mind, meant equal slices for everyone. Then a real morning recalibrated me.

The baby had slept badly and woke with a fever. Two middle kids were arguing about a pencil that belonged to neither of them. A teen had an essay deadline and a face that said, "Please see me." I snapped. My voice was too loud. The room went still. Seven faces looked at me, startled.

I could feel the ache of my own humanity. So I said the only words that could possibly untangle us: "I'm sorry." We prayed at the kitchen table. I told them I needed Jesus just as much as they did. Their shoulders dropped. Mine did too.

That day was not tidy. Dishes crowded the sink. We did less than I planned on paper. We did more than I hoped in the heart. The myth of balance had been quietly stealing joy; presence gave it back. Equal time was never the point. Being truly with the one in front of me mattered more than dividing myself into perfect fractions.

Some seasons tilt toward a child who needs extra support. A teen wrestling through literature and life. A middle child who hits a wall in math. A toddler teetering into a new world of independence that looks, to adults, like serial mischief. Giving extra hours where they are needed is not failure for the rest; it is love in action. Later, the weight will shift, and another will need the front-row seat.

I still plan. I still color-code. But I plan now with an open hand. A mother at our co-op once said, "Balance is a rhythm, not a ratio." That sentence felt like a key sliding into a lock. I stopped guarding minutes like coins and started paying attention to faces.

teaching multiple levels

Grace sets the tone; a little structure makes it sing. Over time we've gathered small practices that keep our many ages thriving without turning the house into a command center.

Rotating focus. Each day I mark one or two children for deeper attention. They know it's their turn to sit closest to me, to have extra eyes on their work, to ask the longer questions. Everyone gets a turn across the week. The others work independently, buddy up, or help a younger sibling. Knowing your turn is coming reduces the scramble to be noticed.

Morning baskets. We keep a basket by age band: picture books and simple puzzles for little hands, copywork and phonics cards for emerging readers, timelines and maps for big kids. When the lamp is on and I'm with someone, the others grab a basket and keep moving. We rotate what's inside every few weeks to keep it fresh.

Staggered starts. Early risers begin sooner and enjoy a longer afternoon. Littles often begin later, after the initial morning bustle settles. This single adjustment cut our interruptions in half.

Short lessons. We aim for focused bursts, especially in the early grades, fifteen to twenty minutes for reading and math, then a break for movement or a new activity. Short lessons invite full attention and protect peace.

Include the littles on purpose. Toddlers and preschoolers want in. Give them chairs, crayons, small responsibilities. A "school binder" with stickers, a zip pouch of chunky beads to string, a stack of wipe-clean cards, a special bin of blocks that only appears during lessons, these small things whisper, "You belong here." They do not absorb all the content; they absorb the atmosphere. That matters.

Buddy time. Pair a big kid with a younger one for ten minutes after lunch. The older reads a picture book, checks a list, or listens to a narration. The younger gets attention that is not rushed. The bond it builds pays dividends you will see years later.

Quiet corners. Noise rises with many people in one space. We've tucked small "nests" into the house: a beanbag under the stairs with a basket of biographies; a window seat with a clipboard and pencils; a porch chair with a lap blanket. When someone needs a quieter space, there's a place to go.

Office hours for older kids. Teens appreciate clear windows when they can find me for uninterrupted help. We block two thirty-minute slots in the afternoon. They plan questions; I show up ready. It respects their growing independence while keeping me from feeling constantly "on call."

Check-ins, not check-boxes. After lunch I do a brief loop, ten minutes with each child to review progress, adjust assignments, and hear concerns. It's enough to keep us aligned without drowning in paperwork.

None of these practices is a magic key. Together they create a gentle spine for the day. Rhythm does the heavy lifting. Grace provides the room to breathe.

that quiet fear of falling behind

Almost every homeschool mother I know carries a tender worry that surfaces at night: *Am I doing enough?* When you teach many ages, the worry can feel louder. You look left and right and imagine other families moving faster, scoring higher, advancing sooner.

I had a season of lying awake, counting the gaps. A son who wrestled with spelling. A daughter who stared at long division like it was written in a code meant for other people. I pictured futures built on the spaces where we hadn't yet arrived, and I felt small.

Then we took a field trip to a living history village. The guide asked about life in the 18th century, and my quiet middle child answered with such thoughtful detail that the guide blinked. She had lived in those books for months, drawn the tools, reenacted chores, baked bread by a fire a dozen times at home. The knowledge had woven into her. It was not quick. It was deep.

Driving home, it settled over me with a kind kind of weight: thorough learning does not always look fast. Growth often hides, then appears in a leap that surprises us both.

When fear creeps in, I use gentle checkpoints that respect the varied pace of a big family:

Portfolios of progress. We keep samples across the year, narrations, sketches, math pages that show corrections, small research notes. Looking back tells a truer story than day-to-day worry.

Conversations. Oral narrations and discussions reveal understanding worksheets miss. Ask, "What surprised you?" "What would you change if you were there?" Curiosity opens more doors than quizzes.

Regular read-alouds. Listening to rich language grows vocabulary and comprehension across ages without separating anyone. The littlest build stamina. The biggest grow insight.

Short skill bursts. When a child struggles, we do five minutes a day on the sticky spot for a month, nothing flashy, just deliberate practice with lots of encouragement. Small daily attention often unsticks what long sessions cement.

One verse steadies me: *"Let us not grow weary in doing good, for at the proper time we will reap a harvest if we do not give up."* (Galatians 6:9) The harvest is not graded on speed. It arrives in due time.

Progress is a patient friend. It shows up while you're washing dishes, reading one more chapter, correcting one more problem kindly. It shows up on a random Tuesday when a child explains a concept to a sibling using an apple and a laugh. The harvest is coming. Keep planting.

sacred interruptions

Somewhere between phonics and algebra, life keeps knocking. A fevered forehead. The washing machine blinking an error code you've never seen. A phone call that changes the afternoon. For a while I viewed these as thieves. Then I watched what they taught us.

When Grandma grew frail, we started writing her letters on Tuesday mornings. The seven-year-old drew daisies with faces. The ten-year-old told her about the garden and the weather. The thirteen-year-old copied a verse in her best hand. We mailed them and marked the calendar. Those Tuesdays became a lesson in compassion, penmanship, and constancy. They also knit us closer to a woman whose stories still anchor our family.

One winter the heater limped on the coldest week of the year. We wore hats indoors and made soup. The kids learned how a pilot light works and how to call a repair company. They also learned gratitude for small comforts. When warm air finally whooshed through the vents, we cheered like we had won a championship.

Our church asked for help with a food pantry delivery on a school day. We loaded the van, carried boxes, and learned how to stack canned goods without buckling a shelf. A volunteer handed my son a clipboard and said, "You're in charge of counting." He straightened. Responsibility has a way of growing a child two inches in an hour.

Many days the right lesson is math. Some days the right lesson is mercy. Both belong to education. I try, each morning, to ask God a simple question: "Show me what matters most today." He is faithful to answer, often with small nudges, a child's tear, a neighbor's need, a chance to pause.

Interruptions no longer feel like detours. They feel like pages in the book we are writing together.

lessons in letting go

Perhaps the hardest work in teaching many ages is releasing the picture of how you imagined it would be. I held tight to a version of myself who never raised her voice, who ran on sleep and leafy salads, who labeled every bin and stuck to every plan. That mother doesn't live here. The real one is softer, a little sillier, and much more in need of grace.

Letting go changed how I measured success. I stopped counting checked boxes. I started paying attention to the peace in our home. Are we kind to each other? Are we practicing forgiveness quickly? Are we making space for wonder? When those answers lean toward yes, our homeschool is healthy even if a lesson rolls to tomorrow.

Life arrives in seasons. New babies slow the pace. Illness asks you to drop everything unimportant. A move reorganizes your brain for months. These are not signs that you should quit. They are invitations to lean into a different rhythm.

In planting season, we scatter seeds, picture books, field trips, new subjects. In growing season, we water faithfully, daily practice, short lessons, patient correction. In resting season, we let roots dig deeper, more read-alouds, simpler meals, lots of walks. The garden still becomes a garden.

A mentor once told me, "Homeschooling is not a race to the finish; it's a relationship that lasts a lifetime." That sentence sits on a sticky note above my desk. It reminds me my children are not projects. They are souls. Education is discipleship, and discipleship happens in the ordinary: tying shoes, setting tables, showing up for hard conversations, reading one more page at bedtime.

When I let go of my timetable, God's care became easier to see. The child who lagged in reading now devours novels quietly on the couch. The one who hated math stays after dinner to solve puzzles with his dad. The teen who doubted her voice reads a poem at youth group, her hands shaking and her eyes bright. We did not force these blooms open. They unfolded while we made room.

the miracle in the middle

A few months ago, after everyone drifted to bed and the house exhaled, I sat at the kitchen table alone. The day had stretched too long. We cried over algebra. We wiped up orange juice that went everywhere. The sink filled itself twice. I held my coffee with both hands and looked around.

Crayons scattered like confetti. A stack of books, some spine-up, some spine-down, waited by the candle. An abandoned timeline card of a Roman road lay under a spoon. The table held the story of our day like a photograph left in a darkroom tray. It was messy. It was alive.

Peace settled in quietly. Not a drumroll. More like a blanket. I remembered the verse that carried me through our first uncertain year: *"He gently leads those that have young."* (Isaiah 40:11) Gentle leading, that is the shape this life keeps taking. Not sprinting. Not dragging. Step by faithful step, together.

I used to believe the goal was to tame the chaos. Now I look for God inside it. I find Him in the patience a sister shows a brother when a concept won't stick. I find Him in the quiet apology a teenager offers after a sharp word. I find Him in the toddler's belly laugh that interrupts a tense moment and saves it. He does not wait for a clean table to join us. He meets us in the middle.

That night I blew out the candle and whispered, "Thank You for today." Not because it was flawless. Because it was ours, and He was there.

love multiplies, not divides

Teaching many ages can feel like slicing yourself into thinner and thinner pieces. But love doesn't thin; it multiplies. A shared read-aloud covers four grades at once. A teen's patient help teaches two people at the same time. A mother's whispered prayer over a child's workbook fills the house with a kind of quiet nothing else can make.

Every small patience, every moment you choose presence, every time you start again after a rough morning, you are building something that lasts. The same grace that multiplied loaves and fish can multiply your minutes, your peace, and your capacity to love.

Perfectly synchronized lessons aren't the aim. Growing together is. One ordinary table. One real family. One beautiful, messy day at a time.

my story: having grace at the big table

If you opened our front door at 8:29 a.m., you would think we run a diner that also sells stationery.

The griddle hisses. Someone shouts, "Where's my pencil?" as if the pencil is a runaway pet. A stack of books leans against a jar of oatmeal like patrons waiting for a booth. Glitter lives inside the wood grain of our kitchen table, a permanent constellation from a craft project that went supernova three winters ago. I used to attack it with vinegar and vigor. Now I call it starlight and take the win.

At 8:30 the whole sky comes in.

The seventeen-year-old arrives first, earbuds draped around her neck, laptop open, a neat stack of notecards for her *Mockingbird* essay. The fifteen-year-old follows, hair in a purposeful bun, clutching a chemistry book and a mechanical pencil that clicks like a metronome. Our ten-year-old, our only boy, slides into his chair with the swagger of a NASA intern and announces, "I like fractions again." The seven-year-old and the four-year-old come in like parade floats, dragging the map of ancient Egypt and arguing cheerfully about whether the Nile looks more like a snake or a zipper. The baby, one and a half, mayor of the kitchen, bangs a wooden spoon on her high chair tray like a gavel. The dog stage-whispers to the cat that he could have been great if not for gravity and rules.

The room hums like a radio tuned to seven stations at once. Somewhere in that hum, learning begins.

"Anchors first," I say, touching the little brass bell by the fruit bowl. We do not keep a clock so much as a rhythm: breakfast, morning time, lunch, quiet reading, dinner. These repeat, even when the weather throws elbows. The teen lights the candle with a match and reverence. We read Psalm 23 because I need it as much as they do. The seven-year-old leans her head on the table and whispers the last line with me: "Surely goodness and mercy shall follow me..." The baby bangs on amen.

"Poem?" the ten-year-old asks. He chooses one with winter fields and black branches. The words put a hush in the room the way snow does. The fifteen-year-old glances out the window an hour later and takes a photo because the sky looks like the poem. That is why we gather first: not to check a box, but to point all our faces in the same good direction before the day scatters us down its hallways.

After the candle, the table becomes a neighborhood. Algebra sets up shop next to phonics. Chemistry leans over paragraphs. Piano practice echoes from the living room because our boy likes to announce his scales to the town. The seven-year-old reads out loud to a stuffed bear and corrects herself kindly; the four-year-old trims paper snowflakes, which is sometimes code for trimming her own bangs. I make a quiet choice not to notice until later.

On my better days, this mess looks like a cathedral.

On my worse days, it looks like proof I am underqualified for my own life.

When we first started, I believed good homeschooling required a clean table, flat surfaces, tidy rows, silence that made pencils sound like crickets. Then one ordinary Wednesday, while I tried for the fourth time to explain why four-sixths simplifies to two-thirds, my oldest slid her chair toward her brother. She didn't sigh. She didn't correct him like a judge. She picked up an apple and a knife.

"Watch," she said gently. "Six slices, then take away two. Same apple. Smaller pieces."

His face found the light, the kind of grin that makes you believe any hard thing can eventually be understood. I stood there, dish towel in my hands, and felt my eyes sting. That quiet exchange said what the neatest room could not: we are forming more than minds here. We are forming patience. Humility. The instinct to help without making a speech about it.

The table is sacred not because it's spotless, but because it holds us all, pancakes, prayers, arguments, apologies. Sometimes we tape copy paper over a sticky patch and keep going. Sometimes we push the books aside and bring out ice water and slices of oranges because the air inside feels heavy. The work of teaching many ages often looks like this, imperfect, honest, alive.

When I remember to breathe and look for it, I hear it under the hum: *This is working.*

Still, there are mornings that feel like a triage line. Who needs me most right now? Who can fly solo for fifteen minutes? Who is melting quietly behind a book?

Early on, I tried to teach every child everything at the same time. I nearly lost my mind and the joy that brought us here in the first place. What steadied me was this: gather where you can; release where you must.

So we start together, Scripture, a short psalm, a prayer that could fit in a pocket. The toddler provides percussion with a spoon. The preschooler delivers crayons like party favors. It still counts.

Then we move into family learning, history and science, the subjects that let everyone touch the same story at their own level. One month we live in pyramids and papyrus, nibbling dates in the afternoon and building a model shaduf by the back steps. The older kids research and write; the younger ones draw and narrate; the littles stick camel stickers in improbable places and watch with big eyes. Another month we move west across a scratch-off map, read pioneer journals, measure flour for cornbread, and watch the way a log yields to fire. Later, when we're planted on the couch, the ten-year-old will ask, "If you had to cross a river, would you float the wagon or find a ford?" and the seven-year-old will answer with alarming gusto. History, I've learned, is better when you can taste it.

Grouping isn't complicated; it's merciful. For the subjects that must be individual, math, writing, upper-level science, we split. I keep a rotation and tell each child when it's their "front-row time." They don't roll their eyes when I say it. They scoot closer. Front-row means I am fully theirs for a spell.

We added small practices to keep the juggle from turning into a circus:

- **Shared first.** The together work rides the morning's fresh energy. It gathers us before scattering us.

- **The lamp.** A small lamp sits on the counter. Lamp on = Mom is with a student; use quiet baskets or independent work. Lamp off = questions welcome. It's astonishing how much peace one lamp can make.

- **Mentor moments.** Big kids aren't little teachers; they're siblings practicing leadership. "Can you listen to her narration?" "Show him how you outline a paragraph." It builds competence on both sides.

One chaotic morning, a crying baby, a long-division disaster, a teen with an essay deadline and that look, I felt the familiar tightening in my chest. A gentle thought landed: *You're not supposed to hold it all. Hold the one in front of you.* So I did. I changed the diaper. I took a breath. I put my hand on the boy's shoulder. "We'll take it one step at a time." The others waited, not perfectly, but patiently enough. Faithfulness often looks like that, the next problem, the next sandwich, the next small mercy.

For years I chased "balance" like a trophy I could earn. If I organized more, tried harder, surely I could meet every need evenly, like slicing myself into precise fractions and serving equal pieces on a tray.

Then a real morning recalibrated me.

The baby had slept like a raccoon and woke with a fever. Two middle kids fought over a pencil that belonged to neither of them. A teen had an essay deadline and eyes that pleaded, *Please see me.* I snapped. My voice was too loud. The room went still.

I felt the ache of my own humanity. So I said the only words that could possibly untangle us: "I'm sorry."

We prayed at the sticky table. I told them I needed Jesus just as much as they did. Their shoulders dropped. Mine did too. The day stayed messy, dishes stacked like a skyline, fewer pages finished than my plan demanded, but we did more than I hoped in the heart. I let go of the myth that equal minutes is love. Presence with the person in front of me mattered more than dividing myself into tidy slices.

Some seasons tilt toward a child who needs extra. A teen wrestling through literature and life. A middle kid who hits a math wall. A toddler practicing independence, which looks to adults like serial mischief. Giving extra to the one who needs it is not neglect of the others; it is love in action. Later, the weight will shift, and another will need the front row.

A mother at co-op once said, "Balance is a rhythm, not a ratio." It felt like a key in a lock. I stopped guarding minutes like coins and started watching faces.

Grace sets the tone; a little structure makes it sing.

Over time, we gathered small practices that keep our many ages thriving without turning the house into a command center.

Rotating focus. Each day two children get deeper attention. They know it's their turn to sit closest, ask the longer questions, work through the knotted parts slowly. Everyone gets a turn across the week, which quiets the scramble to be noticed.

Morning baskets. We keep age-banded baskets: picture books and chunky puzzles for little hands; copywork, phonics cards, and short readers for emerging readers; maps and timelines for big kids. When the lamp is on, baskets come out like quiet invitations. I rotate contents every few weeks so they feel like new toys without the budget or the plastic.

Staggered starts. Early birds begin sooner and earn longer afternoons; littles start after the morning bustle settles. That single shift cut our interruptions in half.

Short lessons. Fifteen to twenty minutes for early reading and math, then up and move. Short bursts invite full attention and protect peace.

Include the littles on purpose. Toddlers want in. We give them chairs, crayons, small jobs. Their "school binder" has stickers and wipe-clean pages; the special bin of blocks appears only during lessons and returns to the closet with ceremony. They don't absorb all the content; they absorb the atmosphere. That matters.

Buddy time. Ten minutes after lunch, a big reads to a little or checks a list or listens to a narration. The younger gets unrushed attention; the older practices gentleness. The dividends compound.

Quiet corners. Noise happens with many humans in one room. We tucked nests around the house: a beanbag under the stairs with biographies, a window seat with a clipboard, a porch chair with a lap blanket. When someone needs space, there's a place to go.

Office hours. Teens get two thirty-minute afternoon windows. They plan questions; I show up ready. It respects independence and saves me from feeling permanently "on call."

Check-ins, not check-boxes. After lunch I do a ten-minute loop with each child: look, listen, adjust. We stay aligned without drowning in paper.

None of these is magic. Together they create a gentle spine. Rhythm does the heavy lifting; grace gives us room to breathe.

Even with rhythm, the quiet worry visits at night: *Am I doing enough?* Teaching many ages can amplify that whisper.

Last spring I lay awake counting gaps like sheep. A son who wrestled with spelling. A daughter who stared at long division as if it were written for other people. I pictured futures built on the places we hadn't yet arrived and I felt very small.

Then we took a field trip to a living history village. The guide asked about winter in the 18th century, and my quiet middle child answered with such thoughtful detail the guide blinked. She had lived in those books for months, drawn the tools, reenacted chores, baked bread by a fire at home. The knowledge had woven into her. It was not quick. It was deep.

Driving home, something settled with a kind weight: thorough learning doesn't always look fast. Growth often hides, then leaps.

Now when fear creeps in, I use humble checkpoints:

- **Portfolios.** We tuck samples across the year, narrations with crossed-out words, corrected math pages, little research notes. Looking back tells a truer story than fretting forward.

- **Conversations.** Oral narrations reveal what worksheets miss. "What surprised you?" "What would you have done?" Curiosity opens doors.

- **Read-alouds.** Shared stories grow language across ages without separating anyone. Littles build stamina; bigs grow insight.

- **Short skill bursts.** Five minutes daily on the sticky spot, with heaps of encouragement. Small attention unsticks what long sessions cement.

"Let us not grow weary in doing good," Galatians reminds me, "for at the proper time we will reap a harvest if we do not give up." The harvest is not graded on speed. It arrives in due time, often while you're washing dishes and a child explains fractions to a sibling using an apple and a laugh.

Somewhere between phonics and algebra, life keeps knocking.

When Grandma grew frail, Tuesdays became letter day. The seven-year-old drew daisies with faces. The ten-year-old reported the weather like a small-town anchorman. The thirteen-year-old copied a verse in her best hand. We mailed them and marked the calendar. Compassion, penmanship, constancy, braided in one small ritual.

One winter the heater limped on the coldest week of the year. We wore hats indoors and made soup. The kids learned what a pilot light is and how to call a repair company. They also learned gratitude. When warm air finally whooshed through the vents, we cheered like we'd won a championship. You can't buy that lesson in a workbook.

On a school day, our church asked for help with a food pantry delivery. We loaded the van, carried boxes, learned how to stack canned goods without buckling a shelf. A volunteer handed my son a clipboard. "You're in charge of counting," he said. My boy stood up straighter, two inches taller in an hour. Responsibility has a way of growing a child where you can see it.

Many days the right lesson is math. Some days the right lesson is mercy. Both belong to education. Each morning, I ask a simple prayer in the pantry where our mission card lives: "Lord, show me what matters most today." He is faithful to answer, through a tear, a neighbor's need, a quiet nudge to pause.

Interruptions no longer feel like detours. They're pages in the book we're writing together.

The hardest work in teaching many ages might be releasing the picture of how you imagined it would be.

I held tight to a version of myself who never raised her voice, who ran on sleep and leafy salads, who labeled every bin and stuck to every plan. She does not live here. The mother who does is softer, sillier, and more in need of grace than any list can fix.

Letting go changed how I measure success. I stopped counting checked boxes. I started watching for peace. Are we kind to each other? Are we practicing quick forgiveness? Is there space for wonder? When those answers lean toward yes, our homeschool is healthy, even if a lesson slides to tomorrow.

Life arrives in seasons. New babies slow the pace. Illness asks you to drop everything unimportant. A move scrambles your brain. These are not signs to quit. They are invitations to lean into a different rhythm.

In planting season, we scatter seeds, picture books, field trips, new subjects. In growing season, we water faithfully, daily practice, short lessons, patient correction. In resting season, we let roots go deep, more read-alouds, simpler meals, lots of walks. The garden still becomes a garden.

A mentor told me, "Homeschooling is not a race to the finish; it's a relationship that lasts a lifetime." That sentence sits on a sticky note above the desk. It reminds me my children are not projects. They are souls. Education is discipleship, and discipleship happens in the ordinary: tying shoes, setting tables, showing up for the hard conversation, reading one more page at bedtime.

When I let go of my timetable, God's care became easier to see. The late reader now devours novels and shushes her siblings. The math-averse child stays after dinner to solve puzzles with his dad. The teen who doubted her voice read a poem at youth group with trembling hands and bright eyes. We did not pry those blooms open. They unfolded when we made room.

A few months ago, after everyone drifted to bed and the house exhaled, I sat alone at the table. The day had stretched long. We cried over algebra. Orange juice went everywhere. The sink filled itself twice. I wrapped two hands around my mug and looked around.

Crayons scattered like confetti. A stack of books, some spine-up, some spine-down, waited by the candle. A timeline card about Roman roads hid under a spoon. The table held the story of our day like a photograph left in a darkroom tray. It was messy. It was alive.

Peace settled quietly. Not a drumroll, more like a blanket. I remembered the verse that carried me through our first uncertain year: "He gently leads those that have young." (Isaiah 40:11) Gentle leading, that is the shape this life keeps taking. Not sprinting. Not dragging. Step by faithful step, together.

I used to believe the goal was to tame the chaos. Now I look for God inside it. I find Him in the patience a sister shows a brother when a concept won't stick. I find Him in the quiet apology a teenager offers after a sharp word. I find Him in the toddler's laugh that interrupts a tense moment and saves it. He does not wait for a clean table to join us. He meets us in the middle.

I blew out the candle. "Thank You for today," I whispered, not because it was flawless, but because it was ours, and He was here.

In the morning, the diner-classroom opens again. The big table gathers us like arms. The lamp clicks on. The bell rings softly. The hum begins.

It still looks like seven stations at once. It still sounds like pencils and patience and someone reading a paragraph aloud in a voice that makes you want to cheer. But now I know the secret that keeps me steady when the glitter catches the light and the baby steals a crayon and the seven-year-old asks if the Nile is a zipper or a snake and the ten-year-old says, "I like fractions again."

And at 11:47, when the dog sighs and the baby claps and the boy finally gets the thing that's been eluding him, I touch the bell and say the sentence that feels like a benediction on our house:

"That's enough for today."

strength for the long road

managing overwhelm & avoiding burnout

Overwhelm doesn't knock loudly. It creeps. It sounds like a pencil snapping in your hand at 9:12 a.m. It smells like burnt toast. It looks like a math page with eraser holes and a calendar with more ink than white space. Most days you can stretch, shake it off, and keep going. Then there are weeks when the edges of everything feel too sharp.

The first time I said, "I can't do this," I was standing in the laundry room with a damp shirt stuck to my wrist and a baby on my hip. The older kids were circling me with questions like moths around a porch light. I didn't need a pep talk. I needed oxygen.

What helped wasn't a brand-new curriculum or a more ambitious plan. What helped was a gentler cadence and some small, faithful practices that brought me back to center.

Name it early. I started listening for my own warning signs: irritability by breakfast, decision fatigue by mid-morning, that tight feeling in the chest when someone says "Mom?" and I want to hide. When those show up together, I call it, out loud if I have to. "I'm getting overwhelmed. Let's slow down."

Return to anchors. We would pull in our day to the bare bones: morning prayer, one skill subject, one shared read-aloud, outside time, and chores. The rest waited. A "minimum day" saved our week more than once. The kids didn't mind. They can feel when Mama's nervous system needs quiet.

Reduce inputs. I paused extra commitments: the new co-op class, an ambitious unit study, even social media for a few days. Fewer voices made it easier to hear God and my own children again.

Make rest visible. We chose a rhythm that told our bodies the truth. A candle during morning time. A five-minute tidy before lunch with music. A fifteen-minute quiet reading break where everyone found a corner. A walk to the mailbox after dinner. Little rituals lowered the noise in my head.

Ask for help. This felt like weakness at first. It wasn't. I told my husband, "I need two hours on Saturday to be alone at the library." He said yes. I texted a friend, "Can you check on me Wednesday?" She did, and she brought muffins. Help usually arrived after I finally said the need out loud.

Pray like a daughter, not an employee. My prayers used to sound like performance reviews: "I tried hard. Please make me better." Now they sound more like, "Father, I'm tired. Lead me gently." Somehow that second prayer leaves me breathing again.

If your season feels heavy, consider a Sabbath week. We've taken a few. No formal lessons. We cook simple meals, read stacks of books, clean the house together, visit Grandma, take slow walks, and get to bed early. It's not quitting. It's recovery. Strangely, we return stronger, as if the soil of our home needed to lie fallow for a few days so new growth could take.

Overwhelm still visits, but it doesn't stay as long. I recognize its voice. I know which doors to close and which to open. And more often than not, joy finds its way back through the small cracks I leave for it.

financial challenges in homeschooling

Our homeschool began with a stack of free library books, a box of crayons, and a budget that made me break out in hives if I stared at it too long. I envied glossy catalogs and felt guilty when I couldn't fill my cart. Then we got creative, and that changed everything.

Start with a simple plan, not a shopping list. Decide what you want to learn this term before you buy anything. One fall we chose: phonics for two kids, writing for one, fractions for another, ancient history together, and nature study. Seeing the targets clearly kept me from chasing every shiny resource.

Use libraries like a second pantry. Our cards did heavy lifting: audiobooks for car time, read-alouds for afternoons, documentaries for rainy days. We learned to request books ahead and pick them up in one swoop. If a title became a family favorite, *then* I hunted for a used copy.

Buy used, and sell what you don't love. Swaps at co-ops, Facebook groups, thrift stores, and library sales gave us treasures for a fraction of the cost. We resold curriculum that didn't fit and used that money to try something new. It felt like our own little scholarship fund.

Share the big things. Microscope? Split with another family and swap twice a month. Expensive science kit? Buy together and rotate the box. Costly field trip? Ask for group rates or choose one anchor trip per term and let the rest be picnics and hikes.

Make what you can. Manipulatives don't have to be fancy. Fraction circles cut from cardstock, a place value chart drawn on a pizza box, number lines made from blue painter's tape on the floor, children learn beautifully with what's on hand. The year we built a cardboard model of the Tabernacle, my kids learned more from a cereal box and gold paint than any kit could have taught them.

Feed the house simply. Groceries were the line that bent our budget. Meal planning rescued me. We rotated five dinners for a month and used a single master shopping list. It wasn't glamorous. It worked. A snack bin with apples, popcorn, and cheese sticks kept surprise expenses from popping up every afternoon in the form of "Mom, we're starving."

Ask for experiences as gifts. Grandparents asked what the kids wanted for birthdays. We asked for museum memberships, zoo passes, pottery classes, and piano lessons. People love giving something that lasts.

Teach kids to earn and steward. The teen babysat for a neighbor and paid for half of her art class. Our middle child made bookmarks and sold them at a church craft fair to fund a field trip. Those small investments made them proud and careful with resources.

We used to think the price tag determined the quality of learning. Now we know better. Good learning sounds like a child saying, "I want to read one more chapter." It looks like a teenager asking, "Can I try to write my own?" It happens at a kitchen table with library books and a pencil stub nearly as often as it happens with something shiny. Some of our richest afternoons didn't cost a cent: a creek, a notebook, a sandwich, and the sky.

facing criticism and doubt from others

If you homeschool long enough, you'll be asked questions in the cereal aisle. Most are curious: "How do you teach algebra?" "Do you have to report grades?" Some carry a different weight: "Aren't you worried about socialization?" "What happens when they need a *real* teacher?" On a tired day, those questions can lodge in your ribs.

We've met critics at family gatherings, from relatives who love us but don't understand our choice. We've heard it at barbecues or in waiting rooms. Some people truly want to know more; some want reassurance that the path they chose is still okay. The difference matters.

I learned a few gentle replies that protect peace:

- "We're grateful to live where families can choose what fits their children. This is working well for ours."

- "We cover academics, of course, and we also get more time for projects, field trips, and service. It suits our kids."

- "Our kids have friends at church, co-op, sports, and in the neighborhood. They see people of all ages, and we like that."

Sometimes I offer a tiny story. "Our daughter learned to read later than the charts predicted. Now she reads on the couch for hours. The slower start let her keep loving books."

If a conversation turns sharp, I remember a simple boundary: *We are the stewards of our children, not the salespeople of our lifestyle.* I don't owe anyone a debate. I can smile and change the subject. I can say, "We're happy to keep talking another time," and hand a toddler a graham cracker.

Doubt also grows from the inside. On a rough Tuesday, I see every flaw magnified: the lesson that flopped, the sibling squabble I handled poorly, the stack of dishes. If I add someone's offhand comment to that pile, it feels like proof. When that happens, I go back to fruit. Are we growing kindness? Are we reading and wondering and becoming? Are we repenting fast and forgiving faster? Fruit tells a truer story than drive-by opinions.

Scripture steadies me. *"A gentle answer turns away wrath."* (Proverbs 15:1) *"As far as it depends on you, live at peace with everyone."* (Romans 12:18) Most people don't need a lecture; they need a calm face and a short, confident sentence.

Years from now, your work will speak. The young adult who writes a thoughtful thank-you note. The teen who shows up early to serve. The child who loves learning long after grades no longer exist. Let your days be your argument. Then put the argument down and go play catch in the yard.

educating multiple children of different ages

We talked about this at length in the last chapter, the table that never stays clean, the hum of many grades, the mercy of rhythm. Here, let's add a few long-haul practices that make it sustainable.

Weekly one-on-ones. Once a week, I take each child for a short "walk-and-talk" around the block or to the porch swing. Ten or fifteen minutes. No agenda, just presence. I ask, "How's school feeling? Anything confusing? What are you proud of?" They tell me truths they wouldn't say in a crowd. Those small windows help me adjust the coming week in ways a planner can't.

A loop for the extras. Subjects like art, composer study, Shakespeare, nature journaling, they add beauty and tend to get bumped. A loop schedule rescued us. After lunch, we simply do the next thing in the loop. If Tuesday disappears into dental appointments, Wednesday picks up where we left off without guilt.

Family work chart. School is smoother when the house runs. We posted a short list of daily jobs right where we can't miss it: five-minute morning tidy, lunch helper, after-lunch reset, dinner helper, evening sweep. Rotations keep it fair. We set a timer and play one instrumental song for each job. The music keeps us moving and reminds me not to micromanage.

Office hours for mom. Two short windows most afternoons when older kids know they can find me for uninterrupted help. They plan questions; I show up ready. It reduces the constant "Mom?" pings and gives the big kids dignity.

Teach what only you can teach. I sometimes ask, "What truly needs my voice?" Reading instruction for a beginning reader? Yes. Feedback on an essay? Yes. A video explaining the Pythagorean theorem for a child who wants to watch it twice? Perfect. Outsourcing strategically isn't failure; it's stewardship.

Protect your soul. A mother is not a machine. When my soul dries up, the house feels it. I keep one book on my nightstand that feeds me, not my homeschool. I write three lines in a journal most nights. I take a walk without earbuds whenever I can. These small habits keep me from becoming a husk in a tidy apron.

Big families look different from year to year. The baby who spilled paint is suddenly reading to a sibling. The teen who needed hand-holding now mentors. Trust that God is growing your capacity alongside your children's. You do not have to be ready for the entire climb, just the next step.

handling days when nothing goes as planned

There are days when you do everything "right" and it still unravels. The dog chews a spelling list. The Wi-Fi falls asleep. You discover at 4:30 that the chicken you planned for dinner is still frozen solid.

We keep a "storm plan" for those days, simple defaults that carry us when the wind picks up.

The three-R reset. Read, rest, and reset the room. We pile on the couch with a good book for twenty minutes. Everyone finds a quiet spot for ten minutes (even if the toddler's quiet spot is a bin of blocks beside me). Then we set a timer for seven minutes and reset one room together, clear the table, sweep, light a candle. The day softens.

The minimum day. One skill subject per child, one shared subject, outside time, and chores. I write it on the whiteboard so my brain stops spinning. Every other box disappears.

Pancakes for dinner. We declared it a family policy: hard days end with easy meals. Pancakes are cheap, quick, and feel like a celebration even when the celebration is "We made it."

Move the body. When tempers flare, I whisper, "Shoes." We walk to the mailbox. We do ten jumping jacks between math problems. We race around the house and come back laughing. Bodies need movement to tell the brain it's safe.

Close the day gently. Bad days tempt me to keep working after bedtime to "catch up." I've learned to do the opposite. I go to bed on time, pray Psalm 4:8, *"In peace I will lie down and sleep, for You alone, Lord, make me dwell in safety."* Tomorrow is kinder when I trust God with what I couldn't finish.

A home that learns how to recover will outlast a home that never stumbles. Recovery is an education all its own.

transitioning from government schools to homeschool

The shift from school doors to your front door is a real change, not just in logistics but in identity. It holds hope and grief at the same time, hope for a new rhythm, grief for what you're leaving. Let both live.

We gave ourselves a "de-schooling" season. That's a gentle way of saying we took time to exhale and remember who we were together. For a few weeks, we woke without alarms, ate breakfast slowly, read aloud, walked trails, visited grandparents, and learned how to be in the same space without bells telling us when to sit and stand. Our kids decompressed. I did too.

Here's what helped that first term:

Talk openly about the change. We named what we were excited about and what felt sad. Our teen missed a favorite teacher. Our middle child missed cafeteria noise (who knew?). We brainstormed ways to keep pieces they loved, Friday lunches with old friends, weekly emails to that teacher, pickup soccer at the park.

Build a simple foundation. We chose three anchors: morning time, a skill subject for each child, and one shared study. Everything else waited its turn. You can add more later. Right now you're building trust and a new muscle memory.

Keep the friendships. Homeschooling doesn't require disappearing. We kept youth group, saw neighbors after school hours, hosted movie nights, and invited a few families over for tacos. It helped everyone remember we changed schooling, not belonging.

Honor their former teachers. We spoke respectfully about the school they left. We wrote thank-you notes. The kids didn't need to hear a campaign speech for homeschooling; they needed assurance that love and gratitude still framed the old season.

Watch for hidden pressure. Children sometimes think they must "prove" homeschooling works. We told ours, "Your worth isn't on trial." We let them settle into a pace that fit, even if it looked slower at first.

Record simply. I kept a notebook with dates, books read, field trips, and a few notes each week. It made the transition feel official enough without swallowing me in paperwork.

After a month, we could feel a new culture forming, more meals together, more laughter, fewer exhausted tears at night. We began to add pieces: math for the one who was ready, a writing program for the teen, a co-op on Thursdays. We still adjust. You will too. Transitions take time, and that time is never wasted.

homeschooling through high school: preparing for college and career

High school felt like a tall cliff until we started climbing it one ledge at a time. It turns out teenagers are fun humans to spend your days with. They drink a lot of milk, ask questions that keep you up at night (in a good way), and want real work that matters.

We sat with each teen at the beginning of ninth grade and asked, "What kind of person do you want to become? What do you want to try?" We made a plan that served the person, not just the transcript.

Credits and courses. We covered the common pillars, English, math, science with labs, history, and a foreign language, then shaped the edges around interest. One daughter loved literature and theater; her credits included a Shakespeare seminar and a season working backstage at a community playhouse. One son fell in love with carpentry; his credits included geometry, physics, and a supervised woodworking mentorship that ended with a table we still eat on.

Transcripts and course descriptions. I keep a simple transcript with course titles, credit hours, and grades. I also write short course descriptions that explain what each class covered and which books or labs we used. It's less daunting if you update it twice a year instead of trying to remember everything at the end.

Labs and experts. For sciences, we used a mix of home labs, co-op classes, and community college dual-enrollment when it fit. A friend who teaches biology invited our teen to two dissection days at her school. People love to share their expertise when you ask kindly.

Testing and timelines. If a teen aims for college, we set gentle timelines for standardized tests and essays, then scale as needed. Practice counts more than panic. Not every path requires testing; trades, entrepreneurship, and creative portfolios open doors too.

Work and service. We encourage jobs, internships, and volunteering. The bakery at the corner taught punctuality, teamwork, and how to handle a rush at 6:30 a.m. Helping at a food pantry taught empathy and logistics. These experiences matured them faster than any lecture I could give.

Mentors. We prayed for adults outside our house who would speak life and truth. God answered. A youth leader who listens well. An aunt who runs a small business. A neighbor who invited our son to help fix engines. Wise voices enlarge a teenager's world.

College and alternatives. Some teens in our circle chose four-year colleges; some chose community college; some apprenticed; one started a lawn care business that paid for his first truck. We try to let the calling drive the path, not the other way around. Psalm 32:8 sits on our fridge during junior year: *"I will instruct you and teach you in the way you should go; I will counsel you with my loving eye on you."*

The best part of homeschooling high school was not the transcript. It was the breakfast conversations, the late-night debriefs after youth group, the way English papers turned into worldview discussions, the way driving lessons became patience lessons for both of us. Your teen wants to be taken seriously and loved fiercely. Give them both.

keeping the joy of learning alive

Joy doesn't arrive with confetti. It's quieter. It hides in ordinary days and asks to be noticed. If you want it to stay, you make a little room.

We keep a few practices that tilt our home toward delight:

Read-aloud culture. Even our teens still wander in when I start a new book. The younger ones color or build quietly while I read. Stories pull us into the same world for a while. They give us common language and private jokes. If the day goes sideways, we call it and read on the couch.

Poetry and tea, simple, not fancy. Once a week, we set out mugs and something sweet. Each person brings a poem, memorized, copied, or read from a book. We take turns. We cheer. The toddler claps for herself after reciting "Twinkle, Twinkle." It's small and it glows.

Wonder walks. We go outside and play "notice three things." A spider web. A cloud shaped like a ship. The way the light turns the ditch grass gold. The seven-year-old notices best. I try to learn from her.

Project weeks. A few times a year we put the curriculum aside and dive into something big. Build a Rube Goldberg machine. Host a family history night where the kids "interview" grandparents with a voice recorder and a list of questions. Create a tiny museum on the dining room table with labels they write themselves. Projects knit skills together and make room for curiosity.

Family exhibitions. On the last Friday of each term, we invite Dad (and sometimes grandparents) to "Exhibition Night." Everyone shares one thing: a paragraph, a painting, a piano piece, a science demo. We eat popcorn and applaud. It isn't a performance; it's a celebration of growth.

A jar of small wins. We keep a jar in the kitchen with index cards nearby. When someone learns something new, conquers a fear, finishes a hard book, or shows extraordinary kindness, we jot it down and drop it in. On New Year's Eve, we read them out loud. The jar tells a story my tired brain would forget.

Keep the heart soft. I watch my own tone. I try to say, "Let's try again," more than "No." I aim for "Tell me what you were thinking," before I correct. Joy and shame don't share the same room. The more I choose kindness, the more joy lingers.

When joy feels far, I return to the simplest remedies: fewer activities, more sleep, sunlight on my face, Scripture in my ears, a friend's voice on the phone, pancakes for dinner, and an early bedtime for everyone. The next morning usually starts with a lighter heart.

strength for the long road

Homeschooling is not a sprint with a medal at the end. It's a pilgrimage with meals, naps, and songs along the way. You will be tired. You will also be changed. The house will carry your laughter in its walls.

On the days when overwhelm visits, pull the day close and breathe. When money feels tight, remember that curiosity is free. When criticism stings, let the fruit of your home speak in time. When many ages tug at your sleeves, choose the child in front of you. When the plan falls apart, make pancakes and read on the couch. When you shift from school to home, give everyone time to become new. When high school looms, take the next ledge. When joy flickers, protect its small flame.

God has not asked you for perfection. He has promised you His presence. The same Hands that multiplied loaves can multiply your minutes and your peace. The same Shepherd who leads beside quiet waters will lead you through noisy kitchens and long algebra pages.

When the house is finally still and the candle smokes a thin line into the air, whisper thanks. You were faithful today. Tomorrow, there will be grace again.

my story: my strength & the long road

The first time I said, "I can't do this," I was in the laundry room with a damp shirt stuck to my wrist and the baby on my hip. The washer hummed like it knew secrets; the older kids drifted in and out of the doorway with questions that sounded like moths bumping a porch light. Someone needed help finding a decimal on a number line. Someone needed scissors. Someone needed me to remember the password none of us would remember in an hour. I wasn't angry. I wasn't even sad. I was empty.

"I can't do this," I said again, out loud this time, so the dryer and heaven could hear me. It wasn't a threat. It was a white flag. And strangely, the moment I surrendered, a thin line of oxygen found me. When you finally tell the truth, there's a little space for mercy to move.

I walked into the kitchen and said the truest words I could to the seven faces looking back. "Mama's overwhelmed. We're pulling in close." I blew out the schedule like a candle. We kept the bare bones: morning prayer, one skill subject, one read-aloud, outside, chores. Everything else waited patiently on the counter like bread dough that could rise later. The kids didn't protest. They could feel the air change too. We called it a "minimum day," and it saved the week.

That night after dishes, I made a small map for my own nervous system. The map wasn't fancy. A candle with morning time. Five minutes of tidy before lunch with one song playing loud enough to drown out grumbles. A fifteen-minute reading rest where everyone found a corner. A walk to the mailbox after dinner, even when the air had that bite that makes you tuck your chin into your coat. Tiny rituals that told our bodies the truth: we are safe; we can go slower; we are still a family.

I told my husband I needed two hours at the library on Saturday, alone with my thoughts and a pencil. He said yes so fast I almost cried. I texted a friend, "Check on me Wednesday?" She showed up with muffins that tasted like cinnamon and survival. I started praying like a daughter, not an employee—less "evaluate me, please" and more "Father, lead me gently." The prayer wasn't long. It was oxygen. And I kept a quiet card in my pocket for emergencies, a line from Isaiah that held my hand: *He gently leads those that have young.*

Overwhelm still visits. It just doesn't stay as long. I know its face now; I've labeled its suitcase. When I hear the pencil snap in my hand at 9:12 a.m. and smell toast going toward charcoal, I name it early and pull us close.

We started homeschooling with a library card and a box of crayons and a budget that made my shoulders creep up to my ears if I thought about it too hard. Glossy catalogs felt like windows into houses where learning smelled like cedar and new paper. Our kitchen smelled like eggs and hope. I learned quickly: the price tag on a book doesn't measure the size of its light.

Instead of shopping our panic, we planned our person. What did *these* children need this term? Phonics for two. Fractions for one. Writing muscles for another. Ancient history together, nature always. The targets shaped the list, not the other way around.

The library became our second pantry. We learned to place holds like pros and pick up a week's worth of wonder in one stop. Audiobooks tucked into drives that used to be silent. Documentaries turned rainy days into small cinemas. When we fell in love with a title, I hunted it used; it was like finding treasure in the wild.

We swapped curriculum at co-op and sold what didn't fit to fund experiments that might. A microscope is expensive—unless you share it with another family and trade on Tuesdays. That fancy science kit? We split it and rotated. The kids learned stewardship without me making a speech.

We used what we had. Fraction circles cut from cardstock; place value on a pizza box; painter's tape number lines that made the hallway look like a track. The year we built the Tabernacle from a cereal box and gold paint, the older kids explained symbolism with such delight you'd think they'd found a hidden door. Turns out they had.

Groceries were our budget's weak knee. Five simple dinners on repeat became mercy disguised as routine. A snack bin served as cease-fire: apples, popcorn, cheese sticks—no negotiating prices with pirates at 3 p.m. When grandparents asked about birthdays, we said, "Museum memberships, please," and suddenly afternoons had a new address. The teens picked up small jobs. A babysitting hour covered half an art class; hand-drawn bookmarks at the church craft fair bought a field trip. They stood taller when they paid for something themselves. There is a certain posture that stewardship makes in a child—it looks a lot like dignity.

The best afternoons still cost nothing: a creek, a notebook, a sandwich, the sky.

Criticism doesn't always arrive with a sneer. Sometimes it's a question asked in the cereal aisle.

"How do they get socialized?" a stranger said, eyeing my cart like it might reveal secrets.

"We're grateful we can choose what fits," I answered, smiling because my seven-year-old was teaching the four-year-old to compare unit prices on oatmeal right behind me. "Our kids have friends at church, co-op, sports, and on our street. They talk to toddlers and grandparents in the same afternoon. It works for us."

At family gatherings, the questions carry more weight because the voices carry love. "What happens when they need a real teacher?" someone asked once, gently. I told a tiny story instead of building a case: "Our daughter learned to read later than the chart said. We didn't panic. Now she reads on the couch for hours, and sometimes I have to tell her to go outside and be human." We all laughed. The air softened.

If a conversation turns sharp, I remember our boundary: we are stewards of our children, not salespeople for a lifestyle. I don't owe anyone a debate. I can say, "We're happy to talk again another time," and put a graham cracker in a toddler's hand like a peace treaty.

The louder criticism usually grows from inside my own head. On a rough Tuesday, some offhand comment will land on top of a flopped lesson and dirty dishes and turn into a verdict. On those days, I go back to fruit. Are we growing kindness? Are we becoming people who wonder and repent fast? Fruit tells a truer story than drive-by opinions. "As far as it depends on you, live at peace," Paul said. Sometimes peace looks like a short answer and then a walk in the cold.

We've already told you about our noisy table—the hum of seven ages like a radio that never quite lands on one station. Sustaining that hum takes longer muscles. We added a few practices for the long road.

Once a week I take each child for a short "walk and talk." Ten minutes, no agenda, the dog trotting like he's got a meeting. "How's school feeling? Anything confusing? What are you proud of?" They tell me truths they won't say with an audience. "I hate copywork." "I think I'm bad at long division." "I love when you read out loud even though I pretend I don't." We adjust the coming week with things a planner can't predict.

Beauty gets bumped by dental appointments if you let it, so we loop it. After lunch we do the next lovely thing: art, composer, nature, Shakespeare, repeat. If Tuesday disappears, Wednesday picks up where we left off without shame. We posted a tiny family work chart where no one can "forget" to see it—five-minute morning tidy, lunch helper, after-lunch reset, dinner helper, evening sweep. We play one instrumental song per job and quit when the song does. Music keeps me from micromanaging and transforms drudgery into choreography.

I keep office hours in the afternoon like a tiny school within a home. The teens arrive with lists; I show up without a phone. Two half-hours where "Mom?" is a welcomed knock, not a background hum. It cut my sense of being permanently on call in half and gave their questions dignity.

And I ask a question as I plan: what truly needs *my* voice? A beginning reader's first steps? Yes. Feedback on an essay? Yes. A Pythagorean theorem video that can be paused and rewound? Perfect. Outsourcing strategically isn't failure; it's stewardship of the only mother they have.

When my soul dries up, the house feels it first. So I keep one book on my nightstand that feeds me, not our homeschooling. I write three lines most nights—what we learned, what I noticed, where God met me. I walk without earbuds often enough to hear my own thoughts again. These are not luxuries; they are the oil that keeps our hinges from squealing.

Some days, for all the planning and prayer, the plan falls apart like a paper crown.

The dog chews a spelling list into modern art. The Wi-Fi goes to sleep and refuses to wake. At 4:30 the chicken for dinner is a glacier. We've learned not to double down on days like that. We run the storm plan.

"Three-R reset," I call, and everyone knows the drill. We pile on the couch and read twenty minutes like we mean it. Then ten minutes of quiet wherever you can find it (the toddler's quiet is a bin of blocks beside me). Then we set a timer for seven and reset one room—clear the table, sweep, light the candle. The room breathes. We do, too.

If the day stays wild, we write four boxes on the whiteboard: one skill subject each, one shared read, outside, chores. Minimum day again. Pancakes for dinner finish it with maple repentance. I put us to bed on time and pray Psalm 4:8 into the pillow: *In peace I will lie down and sleep, for You alone, Lord, make me dwell in safety.* Tomorrow is kinder when I refuse to drag today through its door.

A home that practices recovery outlasts a home that pretends it never stumbles.

The transition from school doors to our front door was its own tender season. We honored it like you would a move or a new baby. For a few weeks we "de-schooled," which is a fancy way of saying we remembered who we were together. No alarms. Long breakfasts. Trails. Grandparents. Learning how to be in the same space without bells telling us when to stand and sit. Our teen missed a favorite teacher; we wrote her weekly emails and sent photos of the books we were reading. Our middle kid missed cafeteria noise (news to me); we hosted Friday lunches with old friends and let the living room buzz.

We started small so trust could grow: morning time, one skill subject each, one shared study. The rest waited on the porch and knocked when we were ready. I kept a simple notebook—dates, books, field trips, a line about the day. It made the new path feel official without swallowing me in paperwork. We didn't speak poorly of what we left; we wrote thank-you notes instead. The kids didn't need a manifesto. They needed to know we changed schooling, not belonging.

After a month, we could feel a culture forming—more meals together, more laughter, fewer exhausted tears at bedtime. We added math where it fit, writing for the teen, co-op on Thursdays. It still moves like a living thing; that's how you know it's alive.

High school looked like a cliff until we got close enough to see the ledges. Teenagers are fun to spend your days with. They drink entire gallons of milk without blinking. They ask questions that keep you up in good ways. They want real work that matters.

We sat with each teen at the start of ninth grade and asked, "Who do you want to become? What do you want to try?" The transcript served the person, not the other way around. We covered the pillars—English, math, sciences with labs, history, a language—then let interest carve the edges. One daughter fell for literature and theater; she did a Shakespeare seminar and worked backstage at the community playhouse, learning timing and teamwork in the dark. Our boy fell hard for carpentry; geometry suddenly mattered because angles become tables, and physics because weight meets wood. A neighbor with a garage and patient hands became his mentor. We counted the hours and the sawdust and called it credit with a straight face and a grateful heart.

Science labs happened at home and co-op and sometimes at a friend's high school when she slipped us into dissection day because she "knew a guy" (bless her). Dual enrollment opened doors when it fit; other doors led to bakeries at dawn and food pantries on Saturdays and engines that woke under a teenager's hands. We prayed for mentors outside our house who would speak life and truth. God sent a youth leader with a kind voice, an aunt who runs a business, a neighbor who fixes things with patience and exactness. Wise voices widen a world faster than any algorithm.

Not every road ends at a four-year college. Some bend through community college, trades, business ownership, missions. We try to let calling drive the path. Psalm 32:8 sits on the fridge during junior year: *I will instruct you and teach you in the way you should go; I will counsel you with my loving eye on you.* That verse steadies everyone—especially me.

The best part of high school wasn't the transcript. It was the breakfast conversations that slid into worldview; the late-night debriefs after youth group; the driving lessons that turned both of us into students of patience.

Joy doesn't arrive with confetti. It arrives like steam from a mug—you have to get close to feel it. If you want it to stay, make a little room.

We keep reading aloud, even though the teens pretend to come for the snacks. Poetry and tea on Thursdays—simple mugs, something sweet, each person bringing a poem or two lines learned by heart. The toddler recites "Twinkle, Twinkle," and bows to thunderous applause; she is certain she is famous. Wonder walks show us the world we live in and often miss: the spider web jeweled with rain; the ditch grass turned to gold; the way the seven-year-old notices everything first.

A few times a year we choose project weeks and shut the curriculum for a while. The Rube Goldberg machine that took over the dining room; the family history night with a voice recorder and a list of questions for grandparents who cried and laughed and told us how the long road looked from where they stood. On the last Friday of each term, we host Exhibition Night: popcorn, one thing shared by each person, applause like a warm coat. We keep a jar of small wins on the counter with index cards and the bossiest sharpie you've ever seen. "Finished long division without tears." "Played piano for Grandma." "Helped sister find courage at the dentist." On New Year's Eve we pour the jar onto the table and read our year aloud. The jar remembers what tired brains forget.

When joy feels far, I cut the extras, guard sleep, find the sun with my face, put Scripture in my ears, call a friend, serve pancakes for dinner, and go to bed early. Joy usually finds the crack that's left.

At the end of a long day, after the candle smokes one thin line into the quiet, I sometimes walk the rooms. A pencil on the stairs. A sock under a chair. A book left open to a sentence someone loved. The house carries our laughter like stitching in the walls. It also carries our tears and apologies and the sound of the bell we ring when the morning begins.

Homeschooling is not a sprint with a medal. It is a pilgrimage with meals and naps and songs along the way. Overwhelm will knock; pull the day close and breathe. Money will feel tight; remember curiosity is free. Criticism will sting; let the fruit of your life speak in time. Many ages will tug; choose the child in front of you. Plans will fall apart; make pancakes and read on the couch. The shift from school to home will ache and heal; give it time. High school will loom; take the next ledge. Joy will flicker; cup your hand around its small flame.

God hasn't asked me for perfection. He has promised me His presence. The same hands that multiplied loaves can multiply minutes and peace. The same Shepherd who leads beside quiet waters leads through sticky kitchens and long algebra pages. When the house finally exhales and I whisper thanks, I hear the sentence that lets me sleep:

Not perfect. Faithful. And tomorrow, there will be grace again.

projects, philosophies, and the wider world

project-based learning

Project-based learning began in our house with a broken toaster. The lever snapped, crumbs everywhere, and seven faces gathered like an audience. The ten-year-old said, "Can we fix it?" The teenager raised an eyebrow but stayed. We found a screwdriver and a YouTube video, laid a dish towel on the table, and met a tangle of springs and a decade of breakfast. We didn't save the toaster, but that afternoon opened a door: questions first, tools second, books third. That order changed our homeschool.

Projects work because they answer a child's favorite question: "Why should I care?" When the goal is tangible, a working machine, a family history documentary, a backyard pollinator garden, theory clicks into place. Fractions matter when recipes double. Ratio and proportion show up in paint mixing. Writing instruction becomes real when the project needs a brochure, an email, or a set of instructions "someone else can follow."

We learned a simple arc for projects: spark, scope, steps, share.

Spark happens in ordinary life. The toddler collects milkweed pods. The middle child wants to know how bridges hold. The teen watches a documentary and says, "I could do that." When you hear the spark, repeat it back: "You're curious about bees." Name it out loud so it grows.

Scope keeps the spark from swallowing the month. Ask three questions together: What will we make or do? How will we know it's finished? What will we need? Write answers on a sticky note and tape it to the wall near the project space. The note becomes a promise you can both see.

Steps break the project into mornings you can actually live. Research two designs. Sketch three ideas. Gather materials. Build a small prototype. Test and note what works. This turns "Make a tiny house out of cardboard" into "Today we draft a floor plan and practice a right angle with a set square."

Share brings purpose. Invite Dad for a five-minute demo after dinner. Record a two-minute video for Grandma. Host a tiny "exhibition night" once a term and let each child show one thing. Sharing teaches children to talk about their work, take questions, and bless an audience.

Our favorite projects looked like this: a backyard bird blind built from pallets and branches; a bread lab that compared yeasts, hydration, and rise times; a family history portrait wall paired with recorded interviews; a neighborhood field guide with hand-drawn leaves and QR codes that link to the kids' audio notes; a small business that printed Scripture memory cards and sold them at church. Each project ran on curiosity and ended in something you could hold, taste, or show.

Faith sits quietly in the middle. When a prototype fails, we pray for wisdom, try again, and notice how perseverance changes the room. When someone shines, we practice gratitude and humility. When a project serves someone else, bee houses for neighbors, a bench for the church playground, it teaches the truth better than any poster: we make because we were made.

educational philosophies & shaping your homeschool

Years ago I tried to pick a single philosophy like people pick a team. I read books with strong opinions and used too many sticky notes. Then I met my actual children. They were not a theory. They were people.

Over time our home grew a blend that fits our family. We borrow Charlotte Mason's love for living books, nature, and short lessons. We admire the classical tradition's attention to truth, goodness, and beauty, along with training the mind to think clearly and speak well. We use Montessori's respect for the child's pace, hands-on work, and prepared spaces where tools have real places. We enjoy the freedom of unit studies and the curiosity of unschooling moments when a question leads the day.

Here's how it looks in our kitchen:

- We read aloud good stories every day. Big kids, little kids, same couch. Narrations afterward, sometimes spoken, sometimes drawn, sometimes acted out by stuffed animals who deserve Oscars.

- We keep copywork, dictation, and recitation in the rotation because beautiful words on the tongue shape more than spelling.

- We set up low shelves with trays: pouring beans into measuring cups for the four-year-old, a bin of magnets and a small whiteboard for the seven-year-old, a simple electronics kit for the ten-year-old. When a shelf looks tired, I freshen it on Sunday night.

- We follow questions. If the seven-year-old asks, "Why does steam disappear?" we boil water and watch the lid. Then we look up the word "condensation" and draw a little picture in a notebook. No pressure to wring a whole unit study from it. We simply honor the moment.

- We loop the "extras": art study, hymns, poetry, composer, Shakespeare, nature journaling. We do the next thing after lunch. No guilt if Tuesday was dentist day. Wednesday is patient.

Philosophies are tools, not bosses. They help you notice what nourishes your particular children. They also give you permission to be a learner with them. The best test is fruit: Are we kinder? Are we curious? Do we end most days with connection still intact? If so, the mix is working.

combining travel and education

When people say "worldschooling," I picture passports and backpacks. Our budget often pictured a minivan and a picnic. It turns out both count.

We started small and close. A Saturday at the Hmong market in St. Paul taught more culture than any worksheet. We listened to languages, tried new foods, and smiled at grandmothers who smiled back. On the drive home the teen googled the history of Hmong resettlement; the seven-year-old rehearsed the names of fruits she could not pronounce but wanted to try again. That day became a page in our family's atlas.

Road trips turned into movable classrooms. We read *Little Britches* while crossing the plains. We stopped at a prairie preserve and walked until wind filled our ears. The kids ran their hands along big bluestem and tried to imagine oceans without water. At Mount Rushmore we talked about art, ambition, and the hard questions they asked when they noticed whose faces were missing.

If you can travel far, wonderful. If you can't, the world still waits nearby. Visit your own city like a tourist. Tour the fire station. Watch glassblowers work. Attend a cultural festival. Eat at a restaurant where you need to ask for help reading the menu and let your kids watch you learn with humility.

A notebook turns trips into learning you can keep. Each child carries a small sketchbook and a pencil. We draw what we see: a doorway, a bowl, a shoe, a skyline. We tape ticket stubs and write one sentence each night: "Today we learned that a buffalo tongue weighs more than you think." We mark maps and pray for the people we met when we get home.

Our faith travels with us. Before we leave, we ask God to make us good guests, slow to speak, quick to listen, eager to honor. We look for a church to visit when we're gone and introduce ourselves like cousins who live far away. We keep Sabbath rhythms even on the road: a slow day for rest and read-alouds on a hotel bed. The world is wide, and the One who made it goes with us.

STEAM at home

Innovation is a big word for what kids do naturally when you give them time, scraps, and a problem. Science, technology, engineering, art, and math already live in your house. You only need to clear a little space and notice.

We turned a corner of the basement into a "build room." It's not pretty. It works. Pegboard with hand tools hung at kid height. A bin of cardboard, a stack of egg cartons, painter's tape, craft sticks, dowels, a small hand drill with a safe bit, a tub of thrifted motors and switches collected over time. On the wall: a simple reminder, "Try three times. Then ask for help." That line changed the way they approached everything.

Science shows up in the kitchen. We ran a bread experiment across a week: four bowls, four yeasts, four temperatures, a daily graph. It became math when they plotted rise in centimeters and compared slopes. It became art when the seven-year-old painted our favorite loaf like a portrait and titled it "Champion."

Technology is not only screens. We counted circuits in our house: doorbells, lamps, toys. The ten-year-old used a battery, an LED, and copper tape to make a light-up greeting card for Grandma. The teen coded a simple quiz in Scratch for the little kids to practice math facts. On a snow day we took apart a broken RC car and labeled what we found. Some days our tech is as simple as a timer that helps us take turns.

Engineering thrives on constraints. "Build a bridge from paper and tape that holds a cup of pennies." The preschooler rolls the paper into tubes. The middle child folds accordion beams. They test, laugh, adjust, and count aloud. The bridge bends just before collapse and they cheer for the edge between strength and failure.

Art belongs in every step. STEAM asks for it. Sketch the design before you build. Choose three colors that make your robot friend look friendly. Add music to your Rube Goldberg machine because joy loves a soundtrack. Creativity is not dessert you add at the end; it flavors the whole meal.

Math is the quiet partner. We measure twice. We mark center lines. We calculate cost per unit with a grocery receipt and argue, in a good way, about which flour is the best buy. I narrate my own thinking when I scale a recipe or budget for a project: "If we have twenty dollars and the dowels cost $1.50 each, how many can we bring home and still buy sandpaper?" The answer matters because the project matters.

Faith meets STEAM in wonder. Psalm 111 says, "Great are the works of the Lord; they are pondered by all who delight in them." When baking soda fizzes, when a seed cracks open, when a circuit finally completes and a tiny light glows, we pause and say thank you out loud. Gratitude keeps innovation from becoming arrogance. It turns success into worship.

entrepreneurship: fostering a business mindset

Our son asked if he could sell lemonade. He wanted to buy a baseball glove and save for a pocketknife like his grandpa's. I saw a summer project and said yes. We sketched a plan at the table, supplies, recipe, a hand-painted sign, and a clean cooler. He learned to count change, greet people, and stand in the sun without slumping. His sisters added cookies and discovered margin when they did the math on butter and sugar.

Entrepreneurship is not only for teens with lawn mowers. It's a posture toward work: notice a need, solve a problem, serve a person, price fairly, show up again. Homeschooling gives calendar room to practice.

We tried small ventures that matched each child's shape. One designed simple bookmarks and sold them at church. Another restored thrifted bikes with a neighbor who loved grease and patience. A teen started a pet-sitting service and kept careful notes on feeding schedules and quirks. We treated these like classes because they were: writing emails, making flyers, tracking expenses in a notebook, counting income, tithing on profit, saving toward a goal.

A few guardrails kept business from swallowing childhood. We kept hours reasonable, honored Sabbath, and insisted on schoolwork first. We said no to growth that outpaced character. Money is a loud teacher; we wanted a quiet classroom.

Mentors helped. A friend who runs a bakery let one teen shadow her for a morning. A dad from church taught our son to write an estimate and follow through. Grandparents told stories about starting small. Teenagers listened because real people beat lectures.

Failures earned a place at the table too. A rainy Saturday ruined the bake sale; we froze leftovers and tried again in two weeks. A client paid late; we learned to write clear terms and follow up kindly. A pet-sitting job went sideways when a dog refused to eat; we called the owner, prayed, and earned trust by being honest. Entrepreneurship in a homeschool is another form of project-based learning with customers. Its best lesson is this: serve people and God will shape your heart as much as your skills.

record keeping and portfolio development

When our oldest reached middle school, I started to worry about records. Worry did not create transcripts; habits did. We built a system that worked on tired days and grew with us.

We keep three layers: daily notes, monthly portfolios, and an annual summary.

Daily notes live in a simple teacher's log. I jot the read-aloud title, skill lessons completed, and any spontaneous learning worth keeping: "Mailman stuck in snow, physics of friction, wrote a thank-you note." It takes three minutes after dinner while the kettle heats.

Monthly portfolios are the heart. Each child has a slim binder or a digital folder, depending on their preference. We tuck in a few samples: a math page that shows corrections, a narration, a drawing from nature journaling, a photo of a project, a list of books read, and a short reflection from the child: "This month I learned... This was hard... I'm proud of..." Those reflections tell the truth more clearly than a letter grade. If a piece is bulky, we take a photo and print it small. Each month's work fits behind one tab. At year's end, you can see growth without digging.

The annual summary is for me. One page per child: courses covered with brief descriptions, field trips, service hours, sports or arts, books we loved, and skills gained. For high school, this morphs into a transcript with credits and course descriptions. For the younger kids, it becomes a sweet record I'm grateful for when I forget everything by August.

Photos help more than we expect. I keep an album on my phone labeled "School Evidence." When a child reads to a sibling, builds a model, plants a row, writes a note, or beams at a finished painting, I snap a picture. At portfolio time, we scroll and choose a few. It keeps record-keeping human-sized and joyful.

We back up digital files in two places and keep paper portfolios on one shelf. When doubt whispers, I pull a binder and remember. The work is there. The fruit is there. God's goodness is printed in pencil and glue.

standardized tests as a homeschooler

Tests are tools, not verdicts. We treat them that way here. If your state requires standardized testing, or if your teen aims for college and the path includes exams, you can prepare without letting anxiety set the tone.

We begin with exposure. A few weeks before a test, we look at the format so it doesn't feel like a surprise party with a Scantron. The teen practices timing with one section at a time. We talk strategy: read questions first on long passages, eliminate obvious wrong answers, mark and move on, return to sticky spots with fresh eyes. We practice filling bubbles neatly because simple things calm nerves.

We keep practice short. Two or three mornings a week, one section at a time, then a normal school day. Courage builds in small sessions. If a section exposes a gap, we spend ten minutes a day for two weeks on that skill. Then we stop. The goal is familiarity, not a new lifestyle.

Test week gets a gentler plan: early bedtime, protein for breakfast, water bottle packed, a pencil case with extras. We pray in the car: "Lord, help us do our best for Your glory. Bring to mind what we've learned. Keep our hearts steady." I tell them what I needed to hear at their age: a test measures a thin slice of skill on a single day. It does not measure wonder, kindness, courage, or perseverance. Those live elsewhere.

If results arrive with surprises, we treat them like data. Where did we do well? Where can we grow? Sometimes the answer is, "You were tired and nervous. Let's try again later." Sometimes it's, "Let's spend a month reading non-fiction articles and practicing summaries." Tests are helpful when they guide instruction; they are unhelpful when they define a person.

Philippians 4 becomes our script during test seasons: "Do not be anxious... present your requests to God... and the peace of God... will guard your hearts and minds." We hold that promise, then sharpen the pencils and show up.

community resources

I used to imagine that homeschooling meant doing everything alone. Then I noticed how happily people share what they love.

The library is our headquarters. Librarians know our names. They pull books when they see our term theme on the request list. The kids sign up for programs I would never think to plan: a bird banding demo, a maker afternoon with a 3D printer, a behind-the-scenes tour that made the ten-year-old want to be a librarian for two hours.

Museums and parks weave into our months. We choose memberships carefully and use them fully: one art museum, one science center, one state park pass. We go often for short visits and let the kids lead. A twenty-minute stop to stare at a single painting is better for our family than a three-hour forced march.

Local businesses open doors when asked kindly. The bike shop let us watch a tune-up. The bakery showed us the morning proof. The print shop taught us the smell of ink and the clatter of collating. We wrote thank-you notes, brought cookies, and returned once a year with new questions.

Church is a classroom that teaches things no textbook can. Youth group, service projects, older friends who become mentors, little ones who need help with their coats, a worship team that welcomes a teen with a guitar and trembling hands. We show up, and the community shows our children what faith looks like in bodies and time.

Co-ops and clubs offer friendship and accountability. We tried a nature club that met twice a month and changed the way we see seasons. 4-H taught leadership and public speaking without calling it that. A small writing circle for teens at our dining room table on Thursday afternoons turned strangers into friends who cheer each other's drafts.

Grandparents carry libraries inside them. We invite them to tell stories, teach recipes, show us how to fix the loose stair. If your family lives far, adopt a grandparent at church. People in their eighties love to explain a hand tool, a hymn, or a headline from 1963 to a respectful audience. Children listen with the kind of quiet you cannot buy.

Community isn't a checklist; it's a posture. We wave at neighbors. We bring soup to the new mom with twins. We rake one extra yard on a windy Saturday. Those choices make a town feel smaller and a child feel larger in the best way.

big work, small steps

Projects lit a spark at our table. Philosophies gave us lenses. Travel, near and far, widened our eyes. STEAM turned scraps into systems. Small businesses taught service. Portfolios told the story the calendar forgets. Tests found their size and place. Community made the world feel generous.

If this chapter feels like a lot, you aren't asked to carry it all tomorrow. Take one small step. Pick a project and write three steps on a sticky note. Freshen a shelf. Plan a Saturday "worldschool" trip within twenty minutes of home. Clear a corner for building. Ask a friend with a skill to teach your child for an afternoon. Print a simple portfolio cover page and label a binder. Email the library about their next program. Pray for the right mentor for your teen.

God multiplies loaves and minutes. He leads gently and gives wisdom when we ask. Most of the big work in a homeschool happens in a small house with a candle on the table and a child who says, "Watch this." You look. You listen. You bless. And slowly, day by day, the work of your hands becomes the work of their hearts.

my story: big work, small house

The toaster quit on a Tuesday. The lever snapped with a sad click, crumbs like confetti on the counter, seven faces circling as if the kitchen had announced a show. "Can we fix it?" the ten-year-old asked. The teen shrugged, but didn't leave. I laid a dish towel on the table, found a screwdriver, and queued a video. Inside: springs, dust, and the archaeology of a thousand breakfasts. We didn't save the toaster. We did find a door. Questions first. Tools second. Books third. That order quietly rearranged our homeschool.

Projects worked because they answered the small, stubborn question kids ask without saying it: *Why should I care?* Doubling a recipe made fractions behave. Mixing paint turned ratio into muscle memory. Writing mattered when it had a job—a flyer, an email, instructions "someone else could follow." We learned a rhythm that fit our life: spark, scope, steps, share.

Spark arrived disguised as ordinary. Milkweed pods in a coat pocket. "How do bridges hold?" at a red light. "I could make a documentary like that," when a teen put down the remote. I learned to say the spark out loud—"You're curious about bees"—so it had a chance to grow.

Scope kept the spark from swallowing the month. *What will we make? How will we know it's finished? What will we need?* We wrote our answers on a sticky note and taped it above the project spot: promise in paper form.

Steps broke "big" into mornings we could live: sketch three plans, gather material, build a tiny prototype, test and jot what worked. Share gave purpose. Five-minute demos for Dad after dinner. A two-minute video for Grandma. A tiny "exhibition night" each term with popcorn and applause that fit in our living room.

The table saw a backyard bird blind from pallets, a bread lab with four yeasts graphing their rise, a family history wall with voice-recorded interviews, a neighborhood field guide—inked leaves, QR codes to the kids' notes—a little business selling Scripture memory cards at church. Some projects tasted like warm crust. Some sounded like a child explaining their work in a brave voice. The best ones served someone else and left the room kinder than they found it.

I tried, once, to choose a single philosophy like you choose a team. Then I met my actual children. They were not a theory. They were people. Our house grew a blend that fit our feet: Charlotte Mason's living books and short lessons, the classical love of clear thinking and beautiful words, Montessori's prepared shelves and dignity of doing it yourself, unit studies when curiosity yanked the wheel, the occasional unschooling day where a question led us by the nose.

Here's how it looked, not on paper but in our kitchen. We read aloud every day—big kids, little kids, same couch. Narrations afterward: told, drawn, or acted by stuffed animals with alarming talent. Copywork and recitation rotated through the week because good words on the tongue change more than spelling. Low shelves held trays that invited small hands: pouring beans, a magnet bin, a basic electronics kit. When a shelf looked tired, I freshened it on Sunday night. Questions were welcome without the burden of launching a unit: "Why does steam disappear?" led to a pot lid, a word—*condensation*—and a tiny picture in a notebook. We looped the lovely things after lunch—hymns, poetry, art, composer, Shakespeare, nature—and simply did the next thing. No guilt if Tuesday vanished into the dentist. Wednesday waits.

"Worldschooling" sounded like passports and backpacks. Our budget often looked like a minivan and a picnic. It still counted. The Hmong market in St. Paul taught more in a morning than a worksheet could in a week. The kids listened to languages, tasted foods I couldn't pronounce, smiled at grandmothers who smiled back. On the drive home, the teen looked up Hmong resettlement history; the seven-year-old practiced naming fruit she wanted to try again. Road trips turned into movable classrooms. We read *Little Britches* crossing the plains, walked a prairie preserve until wind filled our ears, and stood under faces at Mount Rushmore talking about art and ambition and who wasn't there.

When we couldn't go far, we visited our own town like tourists: fire station, glassblowers, a print shop that smelled like ink. Each child carried a small sketchbook. We taped ticket stubs and wrote one sentence at night: "Today I learned buffalo tongues weigh more than you think." Before leaving home we prayed to be good guests—quick to listen, slow to assume.

Innovation lived in our basement corner that wouldn't win an Instagram shoot. Pegboard with tools at kid height. Cardboard bins, egg cartons, painter's tape, dowels, a small hand drill, a tub of thrifted switches. On the wall: "Try three times. Then ask for help." Science happened in the kitchen: four bowls of dough, four temperatures, daily graphs. Math charted rise; art painted the champion loaf like a portrait. Technology wasn't just screens. The ten-year-old made a light-up card for Grandma with copper tape and an LED; the teen coded a Scratch quiz for math facts; on a snow day we autopsied a broken RC car. Engineering loved constraints: paper-and-tape bridges to hold a cup of pennies—tubes, accordions, triumph at the edge of collapse. Art flavored the whole meal—sketch before you build, choose three colors for your robot friend, add music to the Rube Goldberg machine because joy likes a soundtrack. Math ran like a quiet partner: measure twice, mark center, cost per unit at the grocery store, "If we have twenty dollars and dowels cost $1.50, how many and still buy sandpaper?" Faith met STEAM in wonder. When a circuit finally closed and a tiny light glowed, we said thank you out loud.

Entrepreneurship started as a lemonade stand and turned into a class with customers. The boy wanted a baseball glove and a pocketknife like Grandpa's. We sketched supplies, recipe, a hand-painted sign. He learned to count change and stand up straight in the sun. His sisters added cookies and discovered margin when butter costs more than a smile. Another child made bookmarks and sold them at church. A neighbor with patient hands helped restore thrifted bikes. A teen pet-sat with a clipboard of feeding notes and learned to call the owner when a dog refused to eat instead of pretending it was fine. We kept guardrails: school first, Sabbath honored, hours reasonable, "no" to growth that outpaced character. Mentors mattered. A baker let a teen shadow a dawn shift. A dad from church taught how to write an estimate and keep a promise. Money is a loud teacher; we wanted a quiet classroom. The lesson underneath every sale was the same: serve people; God shapes your heart as much as your skills.

When middle school arrived, worry did not generate transcripts; habits did. We built three layers of record-keeping that worked on tired days. Daily notes in a simple log: read-aloud titles, skill work finished, spontaneous learning worth keeping—"Mail truck stuck in snow → friction, wrote thank-you note." Monthly portfolios with a few samples: one math page with corrections, a narration, a nature sketch, a project photo, a book list, and the child's short reflection: "This month I learned... This was hard... I'm proud of..." Those sentences told the truth better than a letter. The annual summary—one page per child—became our memory. For high school it grew into transcripts and course descriptions; for younger kids it turned into a keepsake I'm grateful for when August erases June. I kept a phone album called "School Evidence." When doubt whispered, I scrolled and remembered.

Tests showed up like weather. We treated them like tools, not verdicts. A few weeks out, the teen practiced one section at a time, learned to bubble neatly, to skip and circle back, to breathe. Short practice, normal days. On test week: early bedtime, protein, water bottle, pencils that didn't squeak. We prayed in the car: "Help us do our best for Your glory. Keep our hearts steady." Results were data, not identity. "You were tired. Try later." Or, "Let's read more non-fiction for a month." Philippians 4 guarded our car rides better than any pep talk.

Community turned out to be the secret ingredient. Librarians learned our names and started pulling books when they saw our holds list. A bird-banding demo, a maker afternoon, a behind-the-scenes tour rearranged a Tuesday. We chose memberships carefully—one art museum, one science center, a state park pass—and went often for short visits. Local businesses opened doors when we asked kindly: bike tune-ups, bakery proofing, the smell and clatter of a print shop. We wrote thank-you notes and brought cookies. Church became a classroom too—youth group, service projects, mentors with kind eyes, a trembling teen on the worship team with a guitar. A nature club taught us to see seasons; 4-H taught leadership without naming it; a Thursday teen writing circle at our table turned strangers into editors and friends. Grandparents told stories and taught recipes; when family was far, older friends at church took the grandparent role with delight.

By the end of the chapter, our small house had done big work—one sticky note at a time. If it felt like a lot, we took one small step: pick a project, write three next actions, freshen a shelf, plan a Saturday "worldschool" within twenty minutes, clear a corner for building, email the library, pray for the right mentor. God multiplies loaves and minutes. Most of our big work happens with a candle on the table and a child saying, "Watch this." We look. We listen. We bless. And slowly, day by day, the work of our hands becomes the work of their hearts.

teaching whole people: hearts, minds, bodies & souls

fostering independence and self-directed learning

The day independence started growing in our house, it did not look noble. It looked like me, in yesterday's sweatshirt, whispering, "Ask three before me," while stirring oatmeal with a baby on my hip. We had taped a small card near the table: *try it yourself, check the example, ask a sibling.* Only then, come to Mom.

At first the older kids rolled their eyes. The seven-year-old forgot every step and came straight to me anyway. Still, we kept the little card up and practiced. One morning I watched my ten-year-old stop at step two. He compared his math problem to the worked example, saw the missing negative sign, and corrected it without fanfare. He didn't even look up. I smiled into the oatmeal.

Independence grows when the work becomes theirs. We built a few gentle structures:

We keep **weekly one-page plans** by child, just the targets for the next five days, written in words they understand. No boxes to fill, just a short list they can narrate back. Ownership lives in simple paper.

Each morning we do a **two-minute huddle**: "What will you start with? What might be tricky? Where do you want my help?" They choose the order. I note the hard spots. Then I step back.

We set up **"example corners"**, a binder with one good model of each kind of work: a strong paragraph, a neat math page, a well-labeled nature sketch. When someone asks, "What do you mean by...?" I point to the binder. Seeing a real model makes independence feel possible.

We teach **how** to ask for help: "Show me where you got stuck. Show me what you tried. Tell me your next guess." This turns a vague "I don't get it" into a solvable moment.

Tools matter. A small timer on a desk. Sticky flags to mark questions. A bin labeled "finish later." The older two keep **answer keys** for certain subjects with clear rules, check only after you've tried, circle errors, correct in a different color, and sign your work. Accountability stays firm; dignity stays intact.

Independence also needs room for **self-directed projects**. Our middle child kept a mushroom field journal for a fall. It wasn't my idea, which is why it thrived. She sketched caps and stems, learned a handful of Latin names, pressed a spore print under a glass, and made a simple booklet for Grandma. A project that begins in a child's own question often ends in deeper learning than any assignment I could write.

We aim for a tone that helps independence feel like a gift, not a shove. I say, "You're the kind of person who can figure things out," and mean it. I praise process: "I love how you checked the example and tried again." When mistakes come (and they do), we breathe, correct, and keep moving. Galatians 6:5 sits with us here: *"Each one should carry their own load."* The load is not crushing; it's suited to the person God is shaping.

The fruit has been quiet. I'll find a teenager at the table at 7:10 a.m., already outlining an essay because she likes finishing early. I'll hear a seven-year-old tell the four-year-old, "First we try, then we ask." Independence doesn't make the house silent. It makes the house hum.

social skills

"Hi, my name is Josh. Can I join?" Our son rehearsed those nine words in the van on the way to park day. He wasn't shy exactly; he just liked a script. We practiced smiles and eye contact. We talked about watching a game for a minute to learn the rules before jumping in. When we pulled up, he trotted toward a group at the soccer net, paused, and used the line. The boys shifted to make space. I exhaled.

Social skills are learned the same way algebra is learned, by doing, a little every week, with feedback that doesn't sting. Homeschooling gives time to practice in many rooms: co-op halls, church foyers, library clubs, backyards, and parking lots after youth group.

We keep **circles of belonging**. There's an academic circle (co-op or study group), a service circle (church ministry, food pantry, yard work for neighbors), a play circle (park day, sports, board-game club), and a mixed-age circle (family friends gathered for soup on Fridays). Different circles draw out different muscles. The quiet kid shines where patience is needed. The bold kid learns to listen when the group includes three grandmas and a toddler.

Before an event, we **role-play tiny scripts** in the van. "What's your name?" "What are you building?" "Want to trade?" Afterward, we debrief with "rose and thorn", one good moment, one hard moment. We celebrate attempts, not just victories: "You introduced yourself, even though your stomach did flips."

Hosting helps too. We started **Friday soup and sketch**, a pot on the stove, paper on the table, pencils in a jar. People drop in. Kids draw, trade jokes, and learn not to dominate a conversation because someone's grandpa is telling a story worth hearing. The mess is manageable. The outcomes are enormous.

When conflicts pop up (and they will), we guide without bulldozing. "Ask for what you need with kind words." "Let's try a trade." "Use the timer for turns." And sometimes, "Let's take a breath." James 1:19 is our banner: *quick to listen, slow to speak, slow to become angry.* We model apologies and teach that repair is part of friendship, not proof that it failed.

I used to feel pressured to prove socialization by listing activities. Now I watch for quieter signs: a child offering a snack, a teen seeing a lonely kid and making space, a simple "thank you" to a librarian. Those tell the story better than a calendar ever will.

emotional intelligence & resilience

The morning our seven-year-old called herself dumb, I felt something in me stand up. She had spilled tea on her copywork and burst into tears. The line came out fast and fierce. I knelt and said softly, "Words matter. Let's tell the truth." We named feelings: frustrated, embarrassed, tired. Then we told the story again: "You made a mistake. You can fix it. You are loved." Her shoulders dropped.

Emotional intelligence begins with **naming**. We taped a small feelings chart inside a cabinet door. When someone melts, we point: "What's it like inside?" Naming steals some power from big feelings and gives the brain a way to help.

We keep a **repair ritual** that is simple and real: notice the hurt, name it, own your part, make it right, reconnect. No lectures. A teen who snapped at a sibling might say, "I was stressed and took it out on you. I'm sorry. Want to finish this puzzle together?" Repair teaches resilience because it tells the nervous system, "We can come back from this."

We use **HALT checks** during the witching hour, hungry, angry, lonely, tired. If three boxes are checked, we pause the lesson and tend a body. Sandwiches, a quiet corner, a hug, ten minutes under a blanket with a book, care first, content second.

When a child faces a hard thing, phonics that won't click, a speech at co-op, a lost game, we narrate **growth**, not outcome. "You practiced every day." "You breathed before you spoke." "You kept your tone kind." We might write a tiny note and tuck it under a cereal bowl: "Proud of how you kept going."

Scripture gives us language that heals: *The Lord is compassionate and gracious, slow to anger, abounding in love.* (Psalm 103:8) We say it out loud after a fight. It resets the room.

Resilience is not toughness. It is tenderness with tenacity, soft hearts that keep showing up. We practice by doing one brave thing a week: a new trail, greeting someone first, asking the librarian a question, trying a recipe we've never made. The courage muscle grows quietly, like roots.

And when *I'm* the one who breaks (it happens), I go first with the apology. The kids need to see a mother who knows how to repent and recover. That may be the most transferable skill I teach this decade.

homeschooling as a path to lifelong learning

Our house began to feel different when I stopped presenting learning as something that ends at graduation and started living like a student in front of them. The kids noticed.

I made a **family wonder list** on the fridge: bread baking, watercolor, bird calls, car maintenance basics, a hymn on the piano. Everyone added something. Saturday mornings turned into "try time." Some weeks we watched a fifteen-minute video and practiced a new knot. Some weeks we failed a custard and ate it anyway with berries. The list kept joy in the room.

We hold **"teach us something" nights** once a month. A child picks a topic and gets fifteen minutes to show the family what they learned, card tricks, the history of the saxophone, how to change a bike tire, five sentences in Spanish. Presenting turns knowledge into a gift.

The library card is our passport. Audiobooks in the car, a basket by the couch, a stack by every bed. I stopped apologizing for the hours we spend reading. They are not extras. They are the spine.

We schedule **parent learning** alongside the kids. My husband and I take turns picking a skill to refresh, he rebuilt a birdhouse with our son; I learned to bind a simple book. The kids see us ask questions, make mistakes, and delight in small progress. That matters more than perfect shelves.

Curiosity loves margin. We build **space to meander**: white afternoons with no clubs, slow evenings without screens, Sunday walks with no agenda. A child who is never rushed asks better questions. A mother who is not always in a hurry answers with a kinder voice.

Faith keeps the horizon wide. We tell them often, "All truth is God's truth." The world is full of His fingerprints. Whether we're peering into a microscope or reading a poem, we are meeting the Maker. Lifelong learning becomes worship without needing to announce it.

parental growth

Homeschooling changed my children; it also changed me. I learned algebra again on the floor with a dry-erase board and discovered that my teenage self needed someone to say, "You're smart. Slow down. Try another way." I learned to bake bread that doesn't sink and to apologize without a paragraph of explanation. I learned to sit in silence while a child finds a word.

To keep growing, I guard a few small habits:

A **mother's morning**, fifteen quiet minutes with Scripture and one page of a nourishing book before the house wakes. It's not always serene; someone usually wanders in. Still, my mind starts with truth rather than tasks.

A **pocket notebook**, three lines each night: one mercy I saw, one challenge we faced, one idea for tomorrow. Over months, those tiny records keep me from telling myself a false story about our year.

Mentors on a shelf, I keep a few trusted voices close and ignore the firehose of advice that makes me feel scattered. A short essay that offers perspective will do more for my courage than scrolling ever will.

A **micro-retreat** every quarter, two hours alone at the library to think, pray, look over the kids' work, and name what's working. I come home steadier and kinder because I remembered the point.

Growth sometimes looks like skill. I brushed up on Spanish with a teen and practiced greetings back and forth at the sink. We both mispronounced the same word and laughed. Growth sometimes looks like restraint. I watched a child take longer than I wanted to solve a problem and kept my hands in my lap.

God meets me here. He knows the shape of my limits and loves me inside them. When I feel small, I remember the promise in James: *"If any of you lacks wisdom, you should ask God... and it will be given to you."* I ask out loud. The wisdom arrives most often as patience.

creativity and critical thinking

Creativity rose in our home when I stopped treating it as a reward and started treating it as a way of thinking. It isn't glitter hours and then "real work." It's how we approach any problem.

We keep a **maker hour** most afternoons, nothing fancy, just space where hands are busy while minds wander. Cardboard, tape, string, markers, a bin of odds and ends, music on low. One child builds a tiny stage and scripts a play. Another learns a simple embroidery stitch and teaches her sister. I don't assign outcomes. I guard the time.

Questions fuel thinking. A jar on the table holds slips we've added for years: "What could we invent for rainy days?" "How do bridges hold?", "What makes a joke funny?", "How would you design a city park?" We pull one at dinner and talk. No one grades. The baby bangs a spoon and counts as participating.

We practice **Socratic listening**. When a teenager states a strong opinion about a book or a headline, I ask, "What makes you say that?" and listen for the chain of thought. If the chain has weak links, we name them kindly. We play a simple fallacy game some evenings, spot the slippery slope in a silly ad, find the straw man in a meme. Kids love to catch errors when it's a game.

Constraints spark invention. "Build a marble run on the fridge using only magnets, cardboard, and tape." "Write a poem in eight lines without the letter *e*." "Cook a meal from five ingredients." Constraints make creativity visible and keep projects from sprawling into frustration.

We teach **kind critique** with two questions: "What worked?" and "What could be stronger?" We keep feedback specific. "Your colors guide my eye" beats "It's pretty." "Your argument lost me in paragraph two" beats "It's confusing." Kids learn to receive and give input without flinching.

And we finish things. The last 10% of any project is where character grows, cleaning up files, revising a paragraph, sanding the edges of a wooden box so it doesn't snag a sweater. "Think it. Test it. Tell it." That's our little rhythm. The telling matters because it turns private work into a gift.

physical education and wellness

The year I tried to run P.E. like a coach, it fizzled. The year we turned our family into a moving household, it worked.

We walk a **one-mile loop** most evenings when the weather cooperates. Little legs scooter. Teens talk beside us and forget that they're exercising because they are arguing about plot twists. We wave at the same neighbor with the red hat and count that as community.

Mornings include **movement minutes** between subjects: ten jumping jacks, a wall sit, a balance challenge on a tape line on the floor. The preschooler joins with fierce concentration. The whole thing takes four minutes and changes the room.

We do **seasonal sports** by feel and budget: a rec league in spring, a church basketball team in winter, a backyard badminton net in summer. The goal is joy and stamina, not trophies.

Chores count. A Saturday of raking leaves, hauling sticks, scrubbing the van, and hauling groceries is real work. We name the muscles and call it what it is, strength and service. Kids stand taller when they feel useful.

Wellness is wider than movement. We talk **sleep, water, sunlight, and food** without obsession. Teens learn to read their own bodies. If headaches pile up, we check bedtime and water bottles before we chase exotic causes. We keep simple snacks visible: apples, popcorn, nuts, yogurt, carrot sticks. A family that moves and eats together argues less. It's not science in our house; it's observation.

We treat bodies as gifts. "You are fearfully and wonderfully made" isn't a slogan. It shapes how we talk about shape and strength, about puberty conversations that make everyone blush, about screens that steal hours from the only lungs and legs we'll get. Respect and gratitude are the tone. I ask the girls to thank their bodies after a hike. They roll their eyes and say, "Thank you, knees." Then they laugh and mean it a little.

We keep a simple **activity log** during certain months, not to judge but to notice. Minutes walked, bike rides, stretches held, games played. Seeing the tally grow motivates more than any lecture I could deliver.

arts and humanities

The first time we tried a poetry tea, the toddler dumped sugar in a cup with both hands and declared it soup. We still count that day among my favorites. Art and the humanities open a door to meaning. They turn a house into a home with songs in its walls.

We read aloud every day. Novels, biographies, picture books that do more than entertain. The teenagers wander in when I start a new story, even if they pretend not to care. Stories create a shared language. They give us metaphors when our own words feel thin.

Music plays while we clean. We pick a **composer of the month** and keep it simple: one short bio, one portrait on the fridge, one piece we return to until it feels familiar enough to hum. The aim is affection, not expertise.

Art visits our table through **postcards**, fifty small prints in a box we keep by the candlesticks. At dinner, someone pulls a card, sets it on a tiny easel, and asks, "What do you notice?" We name line, color, mood, and guess titles without peeking. We're often wrong. No one minds. If we make it to the museum that month, we hunt for one painting like old friends and leave after forty minutes while the interest is still warm.

Theater arrives in our living room. We script small plays and let the littles cast themselves as trees if they're nervous. We see one community production a year and talk about the sets and lighting on the way home, not just the plot. The teen who never spoke in co-op auditions for a minor role and grows right in front of us under stage lights.

Humanities include **faith practices** that form us, hymns, psalms, liturgies, church history stories told like family tales. We read one sermon line at breakfast and let it sit all day like a seed.

We also write our own family into the humanities. We interview grandparents with a voice recorder and index cards. We scan old photographs and label names. We make a small "museum" on the dining table once a year with objects and tags the kids write. The humanities stop being far away when you can touch your great-grandmother's rolling pin and hear her tell you about wartime rationing in her own voice.

None of this is fancy. Much of it is fifteen minutes at a time. Over years, those quarters of an hour stack into a life that can recognize beauty and speak thoughtfully about what is good and true.

whole hearts in a living home

Independence grew at the same table where soup spilled. Social skills grew at the park, at church, around a Friday pot of soup. Emotional intelligence took shape in red-faced apologies and quiet repairs. Lifelong learning slipped in when we tried things because we were curious. Parents changed too, page by page, prayer by prayer. Creativity showed up when we gave it time and limits. Bodies grew stronger in loops around the block and leaves raked into mountains. The arts moved in and hung pictures on our walls.

You don't have to build all of this tomorrow. Pick one practice that calls to you. Tape a small "ask three before me" card. Invite one family for soup. Put a feelings chart inside a cabinet. Start a wonder list. Take a slow walk after dinner. Prop an art postcard by the salt. Pray, "Lord, grow us," and mean it.

God is faithful with small seeds. In His time, they become trees that shade your home.

my story: whole hearts in a living home

I ndependence didn't arrive with a trumpet. It arrived as a Post-it.

I taped it by the salt shaker while the oatmeal bubbled: **Ask three before me**, try it yourself, check the example, ask a sibling. Only then, come to Mom. I said it once, quietly, with the baby on my hip. The older kids rolled their eyes. The seven-year-old forgot immediately and came straight to me with a pencil held like an emergency flare.

We kept the Post-it anyway.

A week later I watched the ten-year-old pause over a math problem, glance at the worked example, spot the missing negative sign, and fix it without looking up. No victory lap, no announcement. Just a small, private win. I smiled into the oatmeal and didn't say a word. Independence grows best when it isn't chased.

We drew up one-page weekly plans, five lines and a little breathing room. Each morning, our two-minute huddle: "What will you start with? Where might you need me?" They chose the order. I circled the tricky spots in my head and stepped back. On a shelf we kept a thin "example binder", one neat paragraph, one corrected math page, a labeled nature sketch, so "What do you mean by good?" had a picture, not a lecture. A cheap timer, sticky flags, a bin labeled FINISH LATER: small tools, big dignity.

Independence also needed a field to run in. Our middle daughter fell in love with mushrooms for a fall. Not my idea, that's why it worked. She sketched caps and gills, made spore prints under glass, learned five Latin names she whispered like a spell, and stitched a tiny booklet for Grandma. She did not ask if it counted. It did.

"Hi, my name is Josh. Can I join?" Our son practiced the line in the van on the way to park day, the words packed like lunch. He wasn't shy; he just liked a script. We role-played, eye contact, small smile, watch the game a minute before jumping in. At the net, he said the words. The boys shifted, made space, and the ball moved to his feet. I unclenched my fists and breathed.

Social skills grew by inches, not by speeches. We kept circles of belonging: Wednesday co-op for brains, Saturday pantry for service, Thursday park for play, and Friday soup for a mixed-age mess that felt like church without the bulletin. Before we went anywhere, we tried one tiny script in the van. Afterward we did "rose and thorn" around the table, name a good moment, a hard one. Attempts counted as wins. Hosting helped too: Friday Soup & Sketch, a pot on the stove, paper on the table, a jar of pencils. People came. Kids drew. Someone's grandpa told a story worth leaning in for. We learned that conversation has lanes, and you don't get to hog them.

The morning our seven-year-old called herself dumb, I felt something in me stand up. She had spilled tea across her copywork and grief flooded fast. I knelt and whispered, "Words matter. Let's tell the truth." We opened the cabinet and pointed at the little feelings chart we'd taped inside: angry, sad, embarrassed, tired. She pressed a finger to *embarrassed*, then *tired*, and her shoulders dropped. We told the story again: "You made a mistake. You can fix it. You are loved." Repair lived here too: notice the hurt, name it, own your part, make it right, reconnect. No speeches. "I snapped because I felt rushed. I'm sorry. Want to finish this together?" A sandwich and a blanket often healed more than strategy. HALT checks, hungry, angry, lonely, tired, saved a dozen mornings I would have bulldozed. Psalm 103:8 sat in my mouth like a lozenge: *compassionate and gracious, slow to anger*. We said it out loud after hard moments. The room softened.

We started a wonder list on the fridge the same week the teen asked if learning ends at graduation. "Bread baking, watercolor, bird calls, car maintenance, one hymn on the piano," I wrote. The kids added: "Card tricks. How bridges hold. Bookbinding." Saturday mornings became Try Time. Fifteen minutes, no pressure. We failed a custard and ate it anyway with berries. On "Teach Us Something" nights, a child had fifteen minutes to give the family a new thing, how to change a bike tire, five Spanish phrases, the history of the saxophone. Knowledge turned outward becomes a gift.

I stopped hiding my own learning. I picked up a watercolor brush beside the thirteen-year-old and made two muddy trees before getting one that looked like a tree on purpose. My husband rebuilt a birdhouse with our son; I practiced binding a small book. The kids saw us ask questions, miss, laugh, and try again. They watched me choose patience as often as I could manage it. On a good quarter I took a micro-retreat, two hours at the library with a stack of their portfolios and a quiet prayer: "Show me what's working." I came home kinder.

Creativity rose when it got time on the calendar and guardrails at the edges. We carved a "maker hour" into most afternoons. No assignment, just a table, a bin of odds and ends, scissors, tape, string, markers, music low. One child built a tiny stage and scripted a show. Another taught her sister a knot and embroidered a lopsided star. Constraints kept it playful: "Marble run on the fridge using only magnets, cardboard, and tape." "Write eight lines without the letter e." "Cook a meal with five ingredients." We asked better questions at dinner and listened to the chain of thought: "What makes you say that?" Fallacies turned into a game, spot the slippery slope, find the straw man, and nobody cried when someone said, "Your argument lost me in paragraph two." We finished things too. The last 10% builds character: sanding a box so it doesn't snag a sweater, revising the middle of a paragraph until it says what you meant. "Think it. Test it. Tell it." Our little rhythm.

P.E. worked the year we quit trying to be coaches and started being a moving household. Most evenings we walked a one-mile loop. Little legs scootered. Teens argued plot twists and forgot to notice their lungs working. Between subjects we set a timer and moved for four minutes: jumping jacks, a wall sit, a balance line taped to the floor. In the fall we did backyard badminton; in winter, church basketball; in spring, a rec league if the budget said yes. Saturdays were stealth strength, raking leaves, washing the van, hauling groceries, and we named the muscles like tourists learning landmarks. We talked sleep, water, sunlight, food without obsession. Headaches often solved themselves with an earlier bedtime and a glass of water. "You are fearfully and wonderfully made" wasn't a slogan on a mug; it shaped our tone. I asked the girls to thank their bodies after a hike. They rolled their eyes and said, "Thank you, knees," and then laughed and meant it a little.

The arts moved in with sugar on the floor. Our first poetry tea ended with the toddler dumping a mountain of sugar into her cup and declaring it soup. We still count it among my favorites. Music played while we cleaned. We picked a composer for the month, taped a small portrait on the fridge, and returned to one piece until we could hum along. A box of postcard prints lived by the candlesticks. At dinner, someone propped a card on a tiny easel and asked, "What do you notice?" We guessed titles without peeking and were wrong most of the time. On museum days we hunted for a single painting like old friends, waved when we found it, and left after forty minutes while our affection was still warm.

Theater visited our living room first. We wrote mini-plays and let the littles cast themselves as trees if they were nervous. Once a year we saw a community show and talked about sets and lighting on the way home, not just plot. The teen who never spoke in co-op auditioned for a minor role and grew under lights we didn't own. Humanities reached into the pantry, too, hymns and church history told like family stories. We recorded grandparents with a cheap voice recorder and index cards of questions. Once a year we turned the dining room into a tiny museum with labels the kids wrote, rolling pin, ration book, a photograph with a name we didn't want to lose.

At night, after teeth and prayers and a last glass of water, I walked the quiet rooms and picked up the day: a pencil on the stairs, a page with eraser crumbs, a dried leaf under a chair, an art postcard left by the salt. My pocket notebook took three lines, one mercy we saw, one challenge we faced, one idea for tomorrow. I breathed. Not a perfect day. A faithful one. I thought of Galatians: *each one should carry their own load*, and of the promise that God gives wisdom to those who ask. I asked. I thanked Him for small seeds: a Post-it by the salt, a boy's brave hello, a repair done softly, a loop around the block, a poem read over sugar soup.

In His time, seeds become trees that shade a home.

launching young adults with courage

college preparation

The first time my oldest said, "I think I want to try college," I was rinsing rice and she was leaning against the counter with a pencil tucked behind her ear. We both looked at the pencil like it had answers. It didn't. What helped was breaking "college" into steps we could touch.

We started with a kitchen-table meeting and three questions written on a napkin: What kind of work draws you? What kind of learning lights you up? What kind of life do you hope to wake up to in four years? She talked about biology labs, campus ministry, hiking trails, and professors who knew her name. I wrote fast. We weren't deciding a major; we were learning the shape of a path.

From that afternoon forward, "college prep" looked like ordinary habits done on purpose.

Reading and writing every week. Essays with a clear argument and kind of thesis that could stand up in the wind. Lab-style write-ups for experiments at home or co-op. Emails to adults that sounded like a young professional, not a text thread. She kept a folder called "samples I'm proud of." Later, those pieces became application writing samples and portfolio items.

Math with clean work and real-world uses. We didn't chase speed; we chased accuracy and understanding. When a concept wobbled, we paused and rebuilt it with a whiteboard and patience. When she budgeted for a summer project or compared cell-phone plans, we said, "This is the same math, wearing different shoes."

A transcript that told a true story. Each semester, we logged courses, books, labs, projects, service, and leadership. A parent-issued transcript is accepted by colleges; clarity and consistency matter more than fancy formatting. Twice a year we updated course descriptions, one short paragraph per class, main texts, and how we assessed learning. Future-me was grateful every time.

People who could vouch for character. We asked God for mentors outside our house: a choir director, a biology co-op teacher, a youth leader, the bakery manager who watched her show up early and wash dishes without being asked. When applications asked for recommendations, these adults wrote with specifics because they had seen the work up close.

Campus practice. Long before we toured a university, she took community-college dual-enrollment classes for one or two subjects. She learned to manage a syllabus, email a professor, sit in a lab with people she didn't know, and ask for clarification without shrinking. The credits helped, sure. More than that, they built muscle.

Testing with perspective. Some colleges use test scores; some don't. We checked policies and prepared accordingly: short practice blocks, timed sections, then back to a normal day. On test mornings we ate eggs, packed a water bottle, prayed in the car, and remembered that a bubble sheet measures a thin slice on a single day.

A simple brag sheet. In junior year we kept a one-page snapshot, activities, jobs, service, awards, favorite books, passions. It wasn't for boasting; it was a memory aid for applications and interviews. When someone asked, "Tell me about yourself," she had language ready.

Essays that sounded like her. She drafted in pencil, read out loud to hear the cadence, and cut the parts that sounded like a brochure. In one essay she wrote about failing three times to bake a chiffon cake, then feeding the family the collapsed one with berries and grace. The admissions counselor later said, "That essay made me hungry, and hopeful."

We toured campuses with our senses turned on. Could we picture her studying on that lawn? Did students greet each other in the hallway? Did professors linger after class to answer questions? We paid attention to the bulletin boards, the faith communities nearby, and the distance to a trailhead. On the drive home, we each named one delight and one hesitation. We prayed in the minivan and trusted that the Shepherd who had led us through reading lessons and hard algebra would lead her here too.

career: pathways and preparations

Not every child wants college. Not every calling needs it. The kitchen table can launch a welder, a nurse, a photographer, a software tester, a carpenter, a baker, a missionary, a small-business owner, and a dozen other faithful workers. The work of these years is to help a teenager discover gifts, try real tasks, and meet real adults who do the work every day.

We began with apprenticeship in the old sense of the word: learning by standing next to someone experienced. A neighbor invited our son to shadow him in his workshop, then handed him sandpaper and a block of maple. Another friend, an EMT, let our teen ask questions about training and ride-alongs. A mom at church who runs a graphic-design studio let our daughter sit in on a client call and then try a small layout with feedback.

At home we built "career labs" that matched their interests.

- A "maker lab" for the one who loves tools: measuring, drafting, repairing a wobbly chair, building a crate that actually squares, reading a tape measure with confidence, pricing materials, writing a simple estimate, and cleaning up a workspace like a pro.

- A "health lab" for the one who asked questions about anatomy: CPR certification, volunteering at a blood drive, interviewing a nurse about shifts, keeping a sleep journal, planning meals that fuel long days.

- A "digital lab" for the one who builds on screens: coding basics, spreadsheet skills, file hygiene, documentation, project briefs, and the humility to name bugs without panic.

We taught email like a language. Subject lines that tell the truth. Greetings and closings that show respect. Paragraphs with space between them so a busy adult can read. Attachments named clearly. "Thank you" sent within 24 hours after any interview, even if it was just coffee and questions.

We treated part-time work as a class. On Sunday nights, the teen wrote down the week's schedule, transportation plan, homework slots, and one goal: improve closing shift speed, learn the cash register without help, ask a coworker's name and remember it. Paychecks funded savings, tithe, and one small joy. We talked about taxes at the table with a W-2 and a pencil.

If a child leaned toward trades, we visited training programs and asked about hours, pay while learning, certifications, and pathways to mastery. If a child leaned toward entrepreneurship, we set micro-goals: sell five orders to people you don't know, deliver on time, revise your price after real math, and keep records someone else could read. If a child leaned toward service or ministry, we explored internships with clear supervision and healthy boundaries. No path was "less." Each path asked for character and skill.

Faith shaped the questions we asked: Who does this work serve? What kind of person does this work ask you to become? Where will you need courage? How will you rest and stay human? Work is not identity; it is stewardship. The goal was not a perfect plan at 18. The goal was a young adult who knows how to learn, communicate, and keep promises.

scholarship and financial aid

The money conversation used to make my throat tight. Then we learned to treat funding like a scavenger hunt with a list and a calendar.

We began with the federal form that opens the gate: the FAFSA. We gathered what it asked for, Social Security numbers, tax returns, a short list of assets, and filled it out early in the cycle. The confirmation email felt like a key turning. That form made our child eligible for federal grants, work-study, and certain loans, and it let colleges calculate their own aid offers. It wasn't magic. It was necessary.

Next came the scholarship layers, each with its own flavor.

- **Institutional aid** from the colleges themselves. We read each school's site carefully, ran the "net price" calculator, and looked for merit awards based on grades, test scores (if used), portfolios, leadership, and special interests. We kept notes, because details blur.

- **Local scholarships** in our own town: community foundations, rotary clubs, women's leagues, trade associations, alumni groups, employers, utility companies. These often asked for a short essay and had fewer applicants. We found many posted at the high school counseling office website even though our child learned at home. No one minded when we applied.

- **Field-specific awards** for interests: art, agriculture, IT, healthcare, construction, music. A teen who plays violin can apply for music guild funds even if she doesn't major in music. A teen headed for welding can apply for manufacturing grants that help with tools and certifications. Trade programs often have generous support if you ask.

- **Faith-based and service-based awards** from denominations, mission boards, or community organizations. Some asked for a pastor's reference or documentation of service.

We made one central document with deadlines, requirements, and materials submitted. Every essay got saved in a folder, because one prompt about "a challenge you overcame" can often be tuned for another application. Our teen learned to tell her story with specifics: the months she spent tutoring a neighbor, the summer she balanced work and biology, the way she rebuilt confidence after a failed attempt.

Homeschooled students can absolutely win aid. They apply like anyone else, with transcripts, recommendations, evidence of leadership, and a voice that sounds like a real human. We didn't try for everything; we picked a handful each month. Some said yes. Enough said yes to matter.

homeschool transcript

A transcript is a map. It doesn't need to be fancy; it needs to be clear. Here's the structure that kept us sane and served our kids well.

Header. Student name, address, date of birth, parent/administrator name and contact, school name (we gave our homeschool a simple name), and a line that reads "Official High School Transcript."

Course table by year. Ninth through twelfth grade, each with course titles, the credit value, and the final grade. We used the common credit language: one credit for a full year, half for a semester, lab sciences marked clearly. Titles were plain English, "Algebra II," "American Literature," "Biology with Lab," "U.S. History," "Spanish I," "Studio Art," "Intro to Carpentry." If a course was outsourced, community college, online provider, co-op, we noted it in parentheses.

GPA and credits. Total attempted credits, credits earned, and a cumulative GPA. We used a 4.0 scale, weighted only if the outside program documented it. Honesty and consistency matter here.

Standardized test scores (optional). If the student wanted them included, we added a simple line with date and score. Many colleges see these through official reporting; this line is a courtesy.

Signature and date. Signed by the parent/administrator with the date, plus a small statement: "This transcript is an accurate record of [Student's] high school courses and grades."

Behind the transcript, we kept a **course descriptions document**, one page per year with a paragraph per class describing content, main texts, labs, projects, and how we assessed learning. For example:

Biology with Lab (1.0 credit): A survey of cell biology, genetics, evolution, ecology, human systems. Weekly labs included microscopy, osmosis/diffusion, enzyme activity, and dissections (earthworm, frog). Text: *Exploring Creation with Biology, 3rd ed.* Supplemental videos (Bozeman Science) and field experiences at the local nature center. Assessments: lab notebook (weekly), unit tests (8), research paper on freshwater ecosystems (1200 words).

We also kept a **reading list** (title and author), a **portfolio link** (private Google Drive folder with work samples), and an **activities resume** (work, service, clubs, leadership). Not every college asked for these, but when they did, we could click send without scrambling.

We didn't inflate. We did honor what counted. A child who repaired bikes all summer logged supervised hours and wrote a reflection; some colleges appreciated that as elective credit in applied science or entrepreneurship. A teen who spent two years in youth worship team leadership logged it under arts and leadership; churches run on real work.

You can build this as you go. A ten-minute update at the end of each term saves a mother in the future. She'll want to hug you.

the gap year: opportunities for homeschooled graduates

When our second child finished senior year, she was honest: "I'm not ready to pick a campus yet. I want a year to breathe and build." We nodded and started building a plan together. A gap year is not a pause on life; it's a different kind of education.

We wrote three aims on paper: grow in service, grow in skill, grow in wisdom. Then we sketched a year with real anchors.

Work that teaches. She found a part-time job with early mornings and the need to show up on time even when no one else did. She learned to manage money, handle difficult customers, and be kind when she didn't feel like it.

Service that stretches. She committed to a weekly slot at the food shelf and one Saturday a month with a refugee resettlement team. Faces moved from "those people" to "my friends." Her world got bigger without leaving town.

Study that isn't for a grade. She chose two self-led studies with accountability: church history with our pastor's reading list and watercolor with a local artist who offered critiques once a month. She kept a commonplace notebook and could feel her thoughts deepen.

Travel with purpose. Halfway through the year, she joined a short-term mission trip approved by our church with clear training and debriefing. It wasn't tourism. It was listening and serving. She returned tired and grounded.

Mentors with eyes on her. We asked two adults to meet with her quarterly. They asked hard questions and celebrated growth. When decisions got muddy, she had voices besides ours.

Re-entry plan. In February she revisited the college/career question with new clarity. She applied to two programs, shadowed in both fields, and wrote down what she learned. By April, the next step felt sturdy underfoot.

We set boundaries that protected the year from fuzziness: a weekly schedule, a simple budget, and a Sabbath. Screens didn't get to eat whole days. The point of a gap year isn't to drift. It's to deepen. Hers did.

life after homeschooling

The morning our oldest left for campus, the house sounded too big. Her little brother stood in the kitchen holding a mug like it might tell him what to do next. I hugged him and started the oatmeal. Reintegration is real, for the graduate and for the family.

Our daughter texted that week: "Classes are fine. The laundry room is scary." That told me everything. Academics were familiar; community life was new. We coached by text and phone: introduce yourself to the RA, ask one person to lunch, set a laundry timer, find a church by week three, keep a reasonable bedtime even if roommates don't.

For students entering work or trades, the adaptation looks different. Wake before the sun, protect your body, pack a lunch, learn from the quiet worker who does things right, say the person's name who trains you. Show up early. Bring a pen. Write it down. Ask one good question a day.

For families at home, the table shifts. Younger siblings grieve and also bloom. We make space for both. We let the empty chair feel empty, then we hand the eleven-year-old the map for the next read-aloud journey. New leaders rise when old ones leave.

Holidays become logistics as much as liturgy. We plan arrival and departure, ask about food that feels like home now, and hold loosely to who sits where. We welcome roommates who can't afford a plane ticket and keep a spare blanket in the hall closet. Reintegration works best with a tone of blessing: "We're glad you're here. We'll be glad when you go do your good work again."

For the graduate, church becomes a choice. We pray more and remind less. We ask, "Where did you worship this week?" and listen. If they wobble, we resist panic and keep a seat saved.

Adaptation is a family sport. Everyone gets to practice flexibility, forgiveness, and a little humor when the visiting sophomore brings home laundry that could walk itself to the machine. We light a candle at dinner and ask the same questions we've asked for years: Where did you see God's kindness today? What challenged you? What are you learning to love?

the lasting impact of homeschooling

You won't know the shape of the gift while you're handing out phonics cards and wiping the counter. Years later, you catch it in the corner of your eye and realize what grew here.

Siblings who once argued about markers borrow each other's sweaters and cars. The older one teaches the younger to parallel park and speaks gently because he remembers the first winter he tried. The younger one FaceTimes a big sister to ask for soup advice and ends the call with, "Love you, also, where's the oregano?"

Family jokes that started during morning time still collapse us at Thanksgiving. The hymn you sang every Tuesday surfaces at a hospital bedside and steadies a trembling hand. A grown child corrects herself mid-sentence in a meeting because she learned at your table to choose precise words.

Homeschooling didn't erase conflict. It taught repair. That habit remains: apologies without detours, forgiveness that doesn't keep score, shared work that makes a Saturday fly. It also taught presence. Adult children come home for a weekend, and nobody asks, "What are we going to do?" You already know. A walk. A pot on the stove. A board game. A pile of shoes by the door that tells you the house is holding.

Your marriage carries stories the kids never saw, the late-night budget meetings, the whispered prayers on the back steps, the years when you wondered if this was working at all. One day you'll catch your spouse setting two mugs on the counter while your oldest reads a bedtime story to a child of her own, and you'll trade a look that needs no words.

The lasting impact isn't a single outcome. It's a tone: we are for each other. We show up. We tell the truth kindly. We make room at the table. We keep learning. We let grace have the last word.

reflections and advice for future homeschooling families

If I could sit across from you at a coffee shop, I'd tell you a few things I wish someone had told me in 2021 when we started with a baby on my shoulder and a stack of library books bigger than the toddler.

Begin smaller than you think and more faithfully than you feel. Choose a few anchors, Scripture, a read-aloud, one skill subject per child, outside time, and trust that steady steps build a life. Every term or two, add one thing that brings light.

Let your home have a rhythm that fits your real family, not an imaginary one on the internet. If mornings are chaos, move the heavy work to mid-afternoon and let mornings be chores and read-alouds. If the toddler lives loud, teach the teen how to use noise-canceling headphones and write on the porch for an hour.

Keep short accounts, with God, with your spouse, with your kids. Apologize quickly. Forgive before you feel like it. Laugh whenever you can without wounding someone. Small mercies are the oil in the gears.

Document enough to remember, not so much that you stop living. One photo, one line in a notebook, one file folder per month. Your future self will praise you.

Protect wonder. Even in high school. Read poems on Thursdays. Watch meteors at midnight. Learn one bird call. Memorize a psalm. Bake bread that fails and eat it with berries.

Ask for help without shame. Trade babysitting. Share microscopes. Text a friend, "I'm on the floor of the pantry and it's only Tuesday," and let her bring muffins and a joke. Receive help as if you're a person and not a machine.

When fear shouts that you're behind, measure fruit that grades can't see: kindness, courage, curiosity, perseverance. Ask, "Who are we becoming?" and let that answer guide the rest.

Hold plans with open hands. Children change. So do you. The Shepherd leads. When the path turns, you'll have the muscle you built on ordinary days, the muscle that keeps walking.

At the end of the day, I do one small thing that tells my heart the truth. I stand in the kitchen with the light off and the window bright with the moon. I whisper thanks, sometimes with words, sometimes with tears. Then I go to bed like a daughter who is held.

If you're reading this with a pencil behind your ear and rice to rinse, I'm with you. The kitchen table is a good place to raise a human. The God who multiplies loaves can multiply minutes and courage. He gently leads those who have young. He will gently lead you, too.

my story: after the kitchen table, tears & smiles

T he first time my oldest said, "I think I want to try college," I was rinsing rice and she was leaning against the counter with a pencil tucked behind her ear. We both looked at the pencil like it might answer. It didn't. The faucet hissed; the dog sighed under the table; someone upstairs practiced the same four measures on the piano because that's what you do when you're learning—repetition, then more repetition, then a small door opens.

"Okay," I said, shutting off the water. "Let's break 'college' into pieces we can touch."

We sat down with a napkin because the calendar was buried and napkins are fearless. I wrote three questions: *What kind of work draws you? What kind of learning lights you up? What kind of life do you hope to wake up to in four years?* She talked about biology labs that smell faintly of ethanol, campus ministry, hiking trails, professors who learn your name and say it kindly. I wrote fast. We weren't picking a major. We were learning the shape of a path.

From then on, "college prep" looked like ordinary habits done on purpose. She still read on the couch with siblings sprawled sideways, but now she kept a folder called *Samples I'm Proud Of.* Essays with spines. Lab-style write-ups from co-op that didn't sound like she was apologizing for not being a real scientist. Emails to adults that said "Good morning, Dr. Morales," not "hey." Twice a week we sat with tea while she read a paragraph out loud and trimmed what sounded like brochure fluff. One October morning, she wrote about failing a chiffon cake three times and feeding the family the collapsed one with berries and grace. She rolled her eyes when I said, "That's the essay." She sent it anyway.

Math was slower and sturdier than it had been when she was twelve. We chased accuracy, not speed. When something wobbled, we pulled out the whiteboard and rebuilt it in quiet layers. Then we named math in the wild: comparing cell-phone plans at the kitchen table, budgeting for a summer project with numbers that didn't lie. "Same math," I'd say, "wearing different shoes." She got tired of that line. It kept being true.

The transcript grew in a folder like a garden you water on Sundays. I gave our homeschool a dignified name and typed, *Official High School Transcript* at the top because sometimes you have to talk like an adult to remind yourself you are one. Course titles were plain: Algebra II, American Literature, Biology with Lab. If a class came from an online provider or the community college, I put it in parentheses so future admissions people wouldn't have to squint. Twice a year I wrote course descriptions while the soup simmered—one paragraph, main texts, what we did, how we showed we did it. My future self wanted to hug me every time I remembered to include the labs.

Mentors showed up the way they do when you pray and also tell your friends what you're praying for. The choir director wrote a recommendation that sounded like a portrait. A biology co-op teacher let my daughter stay after class and talk about enzymes and faith and how to keep your wonder when data is dull. The bakery manager sent a text at 6:02 a.m. on a Saturday: *She's early. She's kind to the dishwasher. I'd hire her anywhere.* I cried into my mug, then took a picture of the text and dropped it in the brag-sheet folder we kept in junior year: jobs, service, favorite books, small wins we'd forget in the wind of applications.

Testing came and went like weather. Some schools wanted scores; some didn't. We practiced in short bursts, one section at a time, then closed the book and went back to a normal day. On test mornings we ate eggs, packed a water bottle, and prayed in the car: "Lord, help her remember what she knows, and keep her heart steady." A bubble sheet measures a thin slice on a single day. We said it out loud so the truth could shove the panic aside.

FAFSA night was less mystical than I'd feared. We gathered tax returns and Social Security numbers, set snacks on the table like it was a party, and treated the form like the gate it is. When the confirmation email came, we high-fived and put the snacks away before anyone mistook relief for celebration and ate the whole bag.

Scholarships were a scavenger hunt with a spreadsheet. Institutional aid, local clubs that still met in rooms with coffee pots from the 1970s, trade associations with the kind of fonts that don't get updated because the money is going to kids instead of websites. Our teen reworked the chiffon-cake essay for a "failure taught me" prompt and also wrote about tutoring a neighbor through fractions and keeping her voice gentle when he was fracturing. Some said yes. Enough said yes to matter. One night she answered a call on speaker, and the woman on the other end said, "We'd like to award you the community foundation's service scholarship." My daughter put her head on the table and laughed the kind of laugh that has water in it.

Campus tours taught us to read bulletin boards like anthropologists. We watched whether students greeted each other and whether professors lingered after class. We found the prayer chapel and the trailhead. In one cafeteria I heard a roommate invite another to Bible study in a tone that sounded like an actual invitation and not a club. On the drive home we each named one delight and one hesitation, then we prayed in the minivan at the same stoplight where we have prayed for years about job interviews, surgeries, and the time the washing machine died on Christmas Eve.

Not every child pointed toward a quad. Our son smelled like sawdust one spring and didn't apologize. A neighbor invited him into the workshop and handed him sandpaper and a block of maple: "With the grain," he said. Apprenticeship is just a fancy word for standing next to someone who knows how. Together they built a crate that actually squared. He learned to read a tape measure without faking it, to draft a simple plan on grid paper, to write an estimate that didn't mumble. His first client paid late; he wrote a follow-up that was both kind and clear. "Character," his dad said, passing the salt, "is what you call it when you show up the day after a mistake."

Another child shadowed an EMT and came home quiet, the kind of quiet that says the world is heavier and also beloved. She took CPR, volunteered at a blood drive, started sleeping like sleep mattered because she had met a nurse who works nights. A third child liked screens but not chaos. We built a digital lab out of spreadsheets, documentation, and the humility to name a bug without spiraling. We taught email like a language. Subject lines that told the truth. Files named so someone else could find them. "Thank you" notes within twenty-four hours because adults remember who writes them.

"Some people go now," our second child said at the end of senior year, "and some people need a year to breathe and build." She was right. We planned a gap year that wasn't a drift: a part-time job with early mornings and a manager who meant it when she said "on time," weekly service at the food shelf, one Saturday a month with a refugee resettlement team. Two studies—church history with our pastor's reading list, watercolor with a local artist kind enough to critique without crushing. We asked two mentors to meet with her quarterly and ask hard questions. In February she revisited the college/career fork with a steadier hand. By April, the next ledge didn't look like a cliff.

Move-in day for our oldest smelled like new carpet and nerves. We made her bed, set a lamp on the desk because light matters at 11 p.m., and stood too long in a room that suddenly felt smaller without our elbows. She texted two days later: *Classes are fine. The laundry room is terrifying.* That told me everything: academics were familiar; community life was new. We coached by text: introduce yourself to the RA, ask one person to lunch, set a laundry timer, find a church by week three, keep a bedtime even if your roommate doesn't, call your mother when the world feels too wide or too small.

For the ones who went into work, the adaptation was different: wake before the sun, bring a pen, show up five minutes early, write things down, protect your body, learn from the quiet person who does things right, say the name of the person training you and mean it. The kitchen table had taught communication and repair; the shop taught weight and weather. Both were classrooms.

The table at home changed shape. The empty chair stayed empty on Tuesdays and then didn't feel like a hole so much as a promise. Younger siblings bloomed and grieved in turns. We let them. I handed the map of our next read-aloud to the eleven-year-old and he held it like a flag. Fridays set a place for whoever came home dragging a duffel and a story. Holidays became logistics as much as liturgy—arrival times, roommate who couldn't afford a flight, a spare blanket, a pot that stretched. Blessing became the tone: "We're so glad you're here. We'll be glad when you go do your good work again."

Years in, I started to see the long echo. Siblings who once fought over markers borrowed sweaters and cars without keeping score. The older taught the younger to parallel park and spoke gently because he remembered parking on ice the first winter he tried. The younger FaceTimed from a tiny apartment to ask for soup advice and ended with, "Love you—also, where's the oregano?" Family jokes born during morning time collapsed us at Thanksgiving. A hymn we sang on Tuesdays surfaced in a hospital hallway and steadied a trembling hand. A grown child corrected her own sentence in a meeting because she learned at our table to choose precise words. The habits remained: apologies without detours, forgiveness without tally marks, shared work that makes a Saturday fly.

If I could hand anything to the mother reading this with a pencil behind her ear and rice to rinse, it would be small things that grow. Begin smaller than you think and more faithfully than you feel: Scripture and a read-aloud, one skill subject each, fresh air, lunch, kindness. Build a rhythm that fits your actual people. Keep short accounts—apologize fast, forgive before you want to, laugh whenever it won't wound. Document enough to remember but not so much that you forget to live—one photo, one line, one folder per month. Protect wonder with ridiculous seriousness: meteor showers at midnight, poems on Thursdays, one bird call learned well enough to smile when you hear it at the mailbox. Ask for help without the costume of competence. Trade microscopes, swap babysitting, text a friend "I'm on the pantry floor and it's only Tuesday," and answer when she texts that to you.

When fear shouts that you're behind, measure fruit grades can't see: kindness, courage, curiosity, perseverance. Ask, "Who are we becoming?" and let that answer guide the rest. Plans change. Children change. So do you. Hold the calendar with an open hand and the people with both arms.

On the night our oldest finished her first semester, she called from a patch of sidewalk lit by a streetlamp. "I found a church," she said. "The sermon reminded me of Tuesday mornings." I pictured our kitchen, the candle, the Post-it still crooked on the cabinet from years ago, the table with its permanent constellation of glitter that I now call starlight. I pictured the pencil behind her ear.

After the call, I turned off the kitchen light and stood in the doorway the way I have on a thousand nights. The house breathed. I whispered thanks—sometimes with words, sometimes with tears—for the ordinary steps that became a way. The Shepherd who led us through phonics and fractions led us here too: FAFSA on a Tuesday, an estimate on grid paper, a gap year with early mornings, a laundry room that gets less terrifying, a hymn that finds you in a hallway, a table that keeps making room.

We launched young adults from this kitchen, not perfectly, not without bumps, but with courage and clarity that grew like bread—mixed, rested, risen, shared. And every time I wonder if we did enough, I hear the old promise and believe it again: He gently leads those who have young. He gently leads the ones who are no longer young but still learning how to walk.

saying goodbye, turning off the light over the table

M ost nights end the same way at our house. The dishwasher hums. Crayons hide under a chair. Someone's math book waits at the edge of the table like it plans to finish itself while we sleep. I switch off the kitchen light and the window turns into a mirror. If I lean close, I can just make out the ghost of this whole year, pancakes, phonics, apologies, laughter that shook the walls, the quiet look a child gives when something finally makes sense.

When we started in 2021, I thought homeschooling was a plan. It turned out to be a life. The plan helped, sure, but the life, those ordinary hours full of small choices, did the forming. A candle at breakfast. Psalm 23 read with a baby on my hip. Short lessons with room to breathe. Walks after dinner. Soup on Fridays with friends who feel like cousins. A rhythm that forgave late starts and lost pencils. The slow miracle of watching children grow kinder and braver while I learned to do the same.

I used to imagine an end point where everything clicked and stayed tidy. Then God kept handing me people, not checklists. The teenager who needed time to think out loud. The fourth grader whose hands understood a circuit before his mouth found words. The seven-year-old who cried over a smudged page and learned to tell herself the truth: "I made a mistake. I can fix it. I am loved." The toddler who turned every lesson into a parade and taught us what joy sounds like at close range.

If I could give you one thing to carry out of these pages, it would be a permission slip. You get to build a homeschool that fits the family you actually have. Connection can lead. The clock can serve. Projects can start with broken toasters and end with gratitude. Records can be simple and faithful. Tests can take their size. Community can share its gifts. Your home can hold both ordinary work and sacred interruptions without tearing.

Tomorrow might look like this:

The house wakes slow. Coffee. Oatmeal with brown sugar. A candle lit, a psalm spoken aloud with voices still rough from sleep. Morning time at the table while the baby circles in a zigzag with a wooden spoon. A hymn that carries you a little when the day feels heavy.

After breakfast, the olders move to their corners. One outlines an essay and asks you to read a draft later. One opens a math book and sets a timer for twenty minutes. Across the room, a second grader reads to the four-year-old from a basket of picture books you meant to return to the library and didn't, which turns out to be providence.

At ten, history gathers you again. A map spread wide. A short chapter about a place you've never seen. The ten-year-old builds a quick model from cardboard and tape; the seven-year-old sketches a camel that looks like a friendly cloud; the teen looks up the year and says, "Look what else was happening then." Someone spills water. You hand a towel across the table without breaking the story.

Lunch is loud and fast. Dishes clatter. You take ten minutes with a notebook to jot what happened and what wants tomorrow. The afternoon loosens. A project pulls two kids to the porch with a hand drill and a bin of dowels. The baby naps. You read three pages of a novel you love and fall asleep for five minutes with the book on your chest. No one sets the house on fire.

Later, you walk the one-mile loop. Knees remember hills. Someone tells you a joke they invented, and it almost works. Back home, there's soup on the stove and a neighbor at the door with extra tomatoes. After dinner, a board game on the floor. A last round of "Where did you see kindness today?" Bedtime leans long for one child who needs it. You close the day with a small thank-You you can feel in your bones.

That's a day. Not a perfect one. A faithful one.

If the road ahead feels long, tuck a few small practices in your pocket. Keep Scripture near the table and read a little, even when you're tired. Hold one read-aloud in every season; it stitches your years together. Write down one mercy each night. Ask one mentor to walk with you this term. Leave one afternoon open each week so wonder has somewhere to land.

When fear whispers that you're behind, measure fruit that grades can't name. Did someone tell the truth when it cost them? Did siblings make space for each other? Did a child try again after failing? Did you apologize first? These are the marks of an education that will last.

I have prayed many small prayers in the pantry, some with words and some without. The one I return to most is simple: "Lord, lead gently." Isaiah says He does. He leads those who have young with tenderness, not with a whip. He multiplies loaves and minutes. He plants seeds in Tuesday afternoons and lets them become trees we sit under years later.

One day your table will change. A tall child will back down the driveway in a car packed for campus or a first apartment or the trade they chose with steady hands. You will stand in the kitchen, feel the ache, and know that the ache is part of love. You will set one less bowl on the table and light the same candle and realize that the work you did in these rooms keeps going even when they aren't here to see it. The habits, the hymns, the questions, the way your family says sorry and means it, these travel.

Until then, here we are: mothers with pencils behind our ears and rice to rinse, building a life one ordinary morning at a time. I hope your kitchen fills with the sounds that mean you're doing it, a chair scraping back, a laugh you didn't plan, the soft scratch of a pencil across a page. I hope your house learns the weight of peace and the shape of joy. I hope you feel permission to breathe.

If you need a final liturgy for this work, try this:

Bless this table, Lord – its crumbs and candles, its papers and spills. Bless these minds – curious, stubborn, bright, and still becoming. Bless these hands – small and large, willing to try and try again. Bless this mother – weak and held, learning to walk at Your pace. Teach us to number our days, not to cram them full but to fill them with what matters. Let our home be a place where truth sounds like love and learning tastes like grace.

The light over the table is waiting for morning. So are we.

Good Luck, You Can Do This, & God Bless Always

Jenny H Johnson!

P.S. If you've made it this far, take a deep breath with me for a second.

You did it. You showed up, page after page, not because you had extra time lying around, but because you care deeply about your kids and the kind of future they'll step into.

The truth is, there is no perfect homeschool mom. There is only *you*—with your real budget, real house, real kids, and real limits—choosing, one day at a time, to build something different than the broken system you walked away from. That choice alone is brave. That choice alone is enough to start writing a new story for your family.

My hope is that this book has given you more than just ideas and checklists. I hope it's given you courage—to trust your instincts, to adjust when something isn't working, and to believe that connection at the kitchen table matters more than anyone else's scoreboard. You are not "behind." You are not failing. You are doing holy, unseen work that will echo in your children's lives for years.

And you don't have to do it alone.

If you ever wish you had another mom to bounce ideas off of, talk through curriculum choices, or just say, "Tell me this is normal," I would be honored to be that person for you. I read every message myself.

You can email me at: **JHJHomeSchoolMom@Gmail.com**

If you'd like, put "Homeschooling for Unshakable Futures" in the subject line so I know you're writing from the book. Share your questions, your worries, your wins, whatever you're carrying. I can't promise perfect answers, but I *can* promise a listening ear, honest encouragement, and another mom in your corner who believes your family's future really can be unshakable.

www.ingramcontent.com/pod-product-compliance
Lightning Source LLC
Chambersburg PA
CBHW021203130626
46554CB00005B/1954